I had the privilege of knowin̶ team while we were students at Coiumbia Bible College in the early 1960s. His commitment to the Word and his personal integrity was a real gift of God and played a key role in my preparation as a missionary. Ever since then, he and Anne have been close and precious friends of Carolyn and me. The book *Visiting*, written with Stephen Imbeau, captures the Bob Norris we have always known; it concisely, with a simple style and some humor, provides an excellent model and historical insight for any local church pastor.

JIM FASOLD, retired after serving with
Greater Europe Mission in Spain

Pastor Bob Norris's life, ministry, and unusual spiritual and personality gifts have impacted thousands. Even though an evangelist and teacher, God has also blessed Bob with the heart of a shepherd, a rare but blessed combination. His countless years of teaching God's Word have been powerful and fruitful, as the central core of his service to God and his world. His compassion and focus on outreach—both local and to the ends of the earth—have always brought balance to his continual investment in the lives of local Carolinians.

This book, *Visiting*, written by Steve Imbeau, gives us a glimpse into both the evangelist and shepherd sides of Pastor Bob Norris. *Visiting* is a great read, but also an insightful instruction manual for any church's outreach and visiting program. We love its style and its glimpse into the developing, rich friendship between two such different people. God placed Bob and Steve in disparate roles in life and society, but by "going visiting" together they became such close and dear friends. The many stories or vignettes of all the numerous people they visited, and the situations and questions they confronted, are instructive to read.

Robin and I know you all will love this book. We do.

We also love both Bob and Anne and Steve and Shirley.

PAUL AND ROBIN JOHNSON, founders of World Outreach Fellowship,
Sprint Missions, Envoy International,
Amazon Focus, and ALTECO

Pastor Bob and Dr. Steve have lived a tale worth telling—take a ride with them through twenty-five years of Tuesday visits. God is described in the Holy Scripture as the "God who sees"—meaning he sees us, he knows us, he loves us, he cares for us. Many pastors are happy for guests to come to church—Bob and Steve took church to the guests. They extended the hospitality of God's generous love outside the walls, off the campus, and into the streets and the homes of people looking for faith, hope, and love in God. They took the light of Jesus and the church to their neighbors and city. I believe this is the key to this book and their experience: the outreach of the church and its love and its hospitality to the whole city.

Their adventures make a great read. It's been said there are five gospels—Matthew, Mark, Luke, John, and you—and most people never read the first four. Watch and learn, laugh and cry, and enjoy the ride as Pastor Bob and Dr. Steve take the truth and grace of Christianity to one city through an unforgettable twenty-five-year journey. Not to mention their international trips together.

Visiting entertains while it teaches and instructs and, at times, touches the heart and the soul.

ADAM RICHARDSON, lead pastor, Church at Sandhurst,
Florence, South Carolina

VISITING

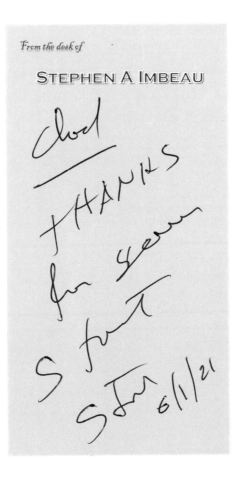

From the desk of

STEPHEN A IMBEAU

Chad
THANKS
for your
Support
S Im 6/1/21

VISITING

Every Tuesday Night

STEPHEN A. IMBEAU

with ROBERT A. NORRIS

credo
house publishers

Published in the United States of America by Credo House Publishers,
a division of Credo Communications LLC, Grand Rapids, Michigan
credohousepublishers.com

ISBN 978-1-625861-99-3

Cover and interior design by Sharon VanLoozenoord
Cover photo by Jozef Polc
Editing by Pete Ford

Printed in the United States of America
First Edition

Library of Congress
Visiting: Every Tuesday Night By Stephen A. Imbeau and Robert A. Norris
LCCN 2021902031 (softcover)
Softcover copy placed with the Library of Congress
US Programs, Law, and Literature Division
Cataloging in Publication Program
101 Independence Ave, SE
Washington, DC 20540-4283

Editorial and historical assistance from Anne and Bob Norris,
Robin and Paul Johnson, Ron Bennett, Angela Head, JoAnne McLaurin,
Pastor Adam Richardson, and other members of the Church
at Sandhurst leadership team.

Scriptural is taken from the King James Version of *The Holy Bible*,
Cambridge University Press, 1979.

CONTENTS

FOREWORD

"ALL MEN ARE CREATED EQUAL" is a cherished phrase bearing witness to a political ideal. All men and women should certainly be treated as equals under the law, but nothing is more manifestly obvious than that we all have unequal endowments and aptitudes.

No one who knows Bob Norris will doubt that he is in the ten-talent category Jesus referred to in the parable. Christians are commanded to be lights in the world. Bob has always been the light in the room. His light has never been hidden under a bushel. We can't always be sure where the boundary is between a personal quality and a spiritual gift, but we have a feeling that Bob's amazing personality was an advantage God conferred at birth. The new birth only enhanced and sanctified what God had already been pleased to give. Although my estimation may seem lavish, it would be difficult to over-compliment Bob.

I am convinced that Bob's winsomeness is rooted in a deep love for Jesus, which shows itself in a radiant and unself-conscious holiness. In the days of the Roman Empire, it was obvious when anyone had visited the perfumer's shop. They brought the fragrance of the place with them. Bob brings the fragrance of Jesus to everyone he touches. Steeped in Scripture, he brings the edification of truth. Intimate in his heart connection to the Savior, he transmits the love of Christ. What he received as a pastoral gift, he improved as a ministry skill by diligent application. He has few equals as a physician of souls. The wedding of great gifts to great humility is the rarest of combinations. We find just such a conjunction in that rare pastor-teacher in Bob.

It was inevitable that his friends would wish to gather their united tributes together in a durable expression of their love and gratitude. So, this book, *Visiting,* only outlines some of the above attributes of Bob, for Steve Imbeau chronicles only one night each week out of seven. Bob was busy every day, making phone calls, writing sermons, studying the Bible, counseling, visiting the sick, spending quality time with family, and dealing with day-to-day church matters during the rest of the week. This book is just a sample, a look at a slice of Pastor Bob's life. But even so, Steve captures the important spirit of the elders, of the deacons, and of all folks at the Church at Sandhurst who poured their love and prayers into Pastor Bob, allowing him the time, the encouragement, the energy, and the enablement to "go visiting" as an evangelist and shepherd. This book is thus a primer of sorts. But this book also can guide any church's pastors and elders to take action, to go visiting. This book is thus also an instruction book on visiting: how to do it and how to approach it. It is my privilege to introduce and endorse the effort.

RONNIE COLLIER STEVENS
Former pastor, First Evangelical Church, Memphis, Tennessee
Former pastor, Danube International Church, Budapest

Ronnie Collier Stevens was a missionary for twenty-four years. He was the first pastor of Munich International Community Church and Moscow Bible Church and the second pastor of Danube International Church, Budapest. You can read his blogs, view his sermons, and order his books at *rampartpublications.com.*

PREFACE

*"For it was not an enemy that reproached me;
then I could have borne it: neither was it
he that hated me that did magnify himself
against me; then I would have hid myself
from him. . . . As for me, I will call upon God;
and the Lord shall save me. . . . Evening,
and morning, and at noon, will I pray, and
cry aloud: and he shall hear my voice. He hath
delivered my soul in peace from the battle
that was against me: for there were many
with me. God shall hear . . ."* PSALM 55:12,16–19A

*"And pray one for another, that ye may
be healed. The effectual fervent prayer of
a righteous man availeth much."* JAMES 5:16

I FIRST MET BOB NORRIS in the summer of 1982, when he and his
wife Anne delivered two fine young men to the University of
Central Florida—an Orlando campus we had rented to launch
a new summer missions program called *"Sprint"* (Summer
Projects in the Tribes). Bob and Anne's son Jeff, along with Jeff
Head, another young man from Harmony Church where Bob
pastored in Sumter, South Carolina, headed off to the scrub
jungles of northern Colombia, South America.

Bob's vivacious passion for Jesus and people instantly connected us, paving the road to an intimate and productive relationship that has lasted these forty years. After Bob and Anne helped three young couples start a church in Florence, South Carolina, I was honored to speak to only 35 people at the first ever Missions Conference at the Heritage Church/Church at Sandhurst. Returning frequently thereafter, we were delighted to watch the church grow. Sandhurst became our sending church, and eventually Bob joined the Board of our mission agency, World Outreach Fellowship.

Pastors do much more than preach. Sometimes they must take action, as shepherds passionately striving to guard and protect and heal their flock. The motto of the Pastor's soul should be: *"Listen up! People will not die on my watch!"* Bob Norris is that kind of Pastor. Robin and I were once crushed by life, and so we've seen this side of a *therapeutic technician* like a Bob Norris.

As the Director of a mission agency, we were unexpectedly attacked by a small number of members, at the very time God was achieving important fruit through our collective efforts in South America. Eventually, our organization merged with another mission agency. We were stunned and wondered what God was doing to us. We fell to our knees crying, as deep waves rolled over our souls and bodies.

Both Robin and I were missionary kids, serving as full time missionaries in South America since 1975; we were mission veterans. Why would God throw away so many years of experience and progress, while seemingly abandoning us? The cries of King David in the Psalms became our cries, our Psalms. See Psalm 55. But then a ray of light. We consulted with Bob Norris and the Church at Sandhurst Elders, and they approved a plan that would bring us to Florence, South Carolina. Their hearts spoke loudly, "We will help you. God is not finished with you yet."

So, in 1995, Bob and Anne Norris welcomed us to Florence, along with church elders Steve and Ann Adams, Bob and Vickye Hinshelwood, and Rob and Deb Colones! Meals and much time alone with Bob and the leadership Elders, allowed us to slowly resolve our agony and bewilderment. These caring people confidentially and quietly nursed us back to health and strength, as Sandhurst genuinely became a *"hospital"* for us. The church members graciously walked alongside us, unwittingly contributing heavily to our restoration. Robin and I have been eternally blessed, through the remarkable years of joint initiative with Bob Norris and Sandhurst.

Shortly after our arrival in Florence, respected physician, political leader and now also an author, Stephen Imbeau coincidentally walked into our lives at a Sandhurst Thursday morning Men's Prayer Breakfast. Sitting directly across the table from me, he listened quietly as I answered questions from different men about our plans to soon move from Orlando to Carolina. He asked about our housing plans. Then, upon understanding our realities, he generously invited us to live in one of his rental houses, recently vacated. The house could not have been more ideal for our needs. Later, he blessed us further by selling us that same house, far below its market value. Steve and Shirley have been long term friends, partners in ministry, and counselors who we respect and highly esteem. Both have been pivotal in our recent ministry projects and continue their crucial impact on our lives. We four all love Chinese food.

Bob Norris and the other elders nursed us back to spiritual and emotional health. We eventually came to understand that God sometimes allows *the death of one dream to* install an even greater dream, a greater mission, for even greater impact. He *"opens up space"* in this way, and then fills it with something that *dwarfs* your original quest—that very place where you *"unwittingly cut your teeth, for much larger pieces of His meat"*—so to speak—see Hebrews 5:12. God showed us the way to a new ministry that would exceed our wildest anticipations. He seemed like the only one *not surprised,* but then, He already knew the end from the beginning and had intervened accordingly!

Once restored and healthy again, we proceeded to help create and develop today's expanding *"Three Waves Movement",* unifying tribal, national and western leaders all across the ten Amazon and lowland countries of South America. In many ways, this new paradigm was *"birthed"* at the feet of the *Sandhurst Shepherds,* who freely allowed our wounded blood to flow through their fingers. They also held us close and constrained us to *fully trust the Father.* It goes without saying, that we owe the stunning blessings of the past 25 years to these men, to their wives, to their Sandhurst initiative, and to their God! One day—before the Throne—*the full story* will be known!

And not only us: Bob's life, ministry and unusual spiritual and personality gifts have impacted thousands. Even though an *evangelist and teacher,* God has also blessed Bob Norris with the *heart of a shepherd,* a rare but blessed combination. His countless years of teaching God's Word have been powerful and fruitful, as the *central core* of his service to God and his world. His compassion and focus on *outreach*—both local and to the ends of the earth—have always brought balance to his continual investment in the lives of local Carolinians. Always upbeat, the Norris family will forever be loved and deeply valued by countless saints and former unregenerate sojourners, whose lives have been massively altered and wonderfully enhanced by these choice children of the King!

This book, *Visiting,* written by Steve Imbeau, gives us a glimpse into both the evangelist and shepherd sides of Pastor Norris. *Visiting* is a great read, but also an instruction manual for any church's out-reach and visiting program. We love its style and its glimpse into the developing, rich friendship between two such different people. God placed Bob and Steve in such disparate roles in life and society, but by "going visiting" together they became such close and dear friends. The many stories or vignettes of all the numerous people they visited, and the situations and questions they confronted, are instructive to read.

Robin and I know you all will love this book. We do. We also love both Bob and Anne and Steve and Shirley.

PAUL JOHNSON
Founder: World Outreach Fellowship, Sprint Missions,
Envoy International, Amazon Focus, and ALTECO

Steve Imbeau and Bob Norris, 2021

INTRODUCTION

"And daily in the temple, and in every house, they ceased not to teach and preach Jesus Christ." ACTS 5:42

"A man that hath friends must shew himself friendly: and there is a friend that sticketh closer than a brother." PROVERBS 18:24

WHAT'S A "VISIT"? Well, the English word means many things: a trip, a "look-see," going to a specific place (i.e., a visit to the store), people getting together (i.e., "I want to visit your family"), a part of a funeral (visitation), an appearance (we were visited by an angel), and then there is *this* kind of visit.

This book is about church visits to follow up on the curious or the interested who came to the Church at Sandhurst in Florence, South Carolina, for a "look-see" or to "check it out" as visitors some Sunday morning. From 1986 to 2013, Bob Norris was the lead pastor at the Heritage Church—which later became the Church at Sandhurst in 1990. In 2013, he partially retired and moved over to the Church at King Avenue, succeeded at Sandhurst by Pastor Adam Richardson in 2015.

Pastor Bob and I began visiting for the church sometime in 1988, continuing on week after week until about 2013. Through thick and thin, rain or shine (well, not as much rain), personal ups and downs, and business losses or gains, we went visiting for about 750 visiting nights and with about 2,200 couples. Wow. We learned a lot and we bonded a lot.

Our primary mission was to meet potential parishioners, encourage them, evangelize them, and establish direct church contact with them. But along the way, we also became dear and close friends. We came to lean on each other, encourage each other, admire each other, counsel each other, and thus become important in each other's lives. And after visiting with almost 2,200 couples, we came to better appreciate humanity, its diversity, its shapes, its personalities, its humor, and its great stories.

So, this book is really about five things: evangelism, church growth, human experience, great stories, and a deep, deep friendship.

We hope you can both enjoy it and learn from it.

Come visiting with us.

VISITING

Every Tuesday Night

Steve Imbeau and Bob Norris in 1999

The Beginnings

*"And I say also unto thee, that thou
art Peter, and upon this rock I will build
my church; and the gates of hell shall
not prevail against it."* MATTHEW 16:18

*"Feed the flock of God which is among you,
taking the oversight thereof . . . neither as
being lords over God's heritage, but being
examples to the flock."* 1 PETER 5:2–3

PATRICIA (ANNE) RUSSELL, was born on October 5, 1938, in Sumter, South Carolina, where she grew up. She later moved to Florence with her father's work and to Columbia for school and work. While a student at Columbia Bible College, she met incoming student Robert (Bob) Norris from Canada and fell madly in love. Anne worked most of her life as a schoolteacher, often in special education classes.

Robert (Bob) Arthur Norris was born on April 7, 1938, in London, Ontario. He grew up in London, turning to his wild nature after his mother died in a car accident; he moved in with his grandmother when his father could no longer provide discipline and decided to turn Bob over to her. Eventually, he became a Christian through his grandmother's faithfulness and prayers. He decided to go to Columbia Bible College after high school, but after an interview in Columbia, decided to work instead, but came back a year later with Les Hobbins, where—lo and behold—a certain Anna was still a student. Anne and Bob were married June 2, 1961, in Sumter.

Graduating in 1962, Anne and Bob then moved around a bit as he became a pastor: to Charlotte at Calvary Presbyterian Church, then to Chicago to study music, then to Shreveport, Louisiana, at the Coventry Baptist Church, then to the Liberty Baptist Church in Appomattox, Virginia, then to the Long Branch Baptist Church in Sumter, then to join the Canadian Barry Moore's evangelism crusade as director of music, then back to Sumter to be the lead pastor at the Harmony Church for many years. Finally, a brief stay in Atlanta followed by a long stay in Florence.

The Norrises' move to Florence has an interesting history. Bob had met Harold Morris at the Georgia State Penitentiary with Bobby Richardson (from Sumter, South Carolina, the former New York Yankees star baseball player) and was part of the Christian team that mentored Harold and worked on his prison release. Harold was convicted and sentenced to two lifelong terms (called a "double elbow" in "prison slang") in the Georgia State Penitentiary as both the mastermind and an accessory to murder during a 1967 Atlanta convenience store hold up, wherein a bystander was shot while pulling a gun on the robbers; Harold was outside as the getaway driver. About eight years later, Harold was saved in prison through his brother Carl and the prison ministry of Chuck Colson, Clebe McClary, and others.

Eventually, free on parole in 1978 and then with a commutation in 1981 by Governor George Bushee, Harold settled in the Atlanta area, even though growing up in Sumter and Georgetown, South Carolina. He was unable to reconcile with some of his South Carolina family and he also had major support from the Cathy family of Chick-fil-A fame. Harold then persuaded a group of Atlanta Christians to organize and invite Bob to be their pastor. So, Bob and Anne both left their jobs in Sumter, South Carolina, and moved to Atlanta, but the new church soon fell apart over internal disputes and immorality. Harold went on to become a noted speaker as an evangelist and counselor to teenagers for about twenty years and the writer of the book and movie *Twice Pardoned*, outlining his life story. Harold was honored by President George H. W. Bush with a Points of Light award for 1992–93; Bob O'Harra and I went up for the banquet at the DC Hilton with Harold, sitting at the Cathy family table along with Gary and Carol Bauer (he of *Focus on the Family* and a future presidential candidate). Harold was a contributor to the Church at Sandhurst with one major behest as a matching gift to assist the original land purchase along Third Loop Road in Florence; his challenge to raise money from the Sandhurst congregation in the YMCA gymnasium is unforgettable. Harold died on June 14, 2017, and Sandhurst elder Bob Hinshelwood attended his funeral in Clayton, Georgia.

At the same time, Rob and Deb Colones—Rob came from Sumter and was saved through Pastor Bob's former Sumter Harmony Church—were trying to start a Bible fellowship church in Florence along with Dr. Steve and Ann Adams and Bob and Vickye Hinshelwood. Starting in late 1984, Pastor Bob came over from Sumter to hold weekly Bible studies and hymn sings in the couples' homes and later also in Marianne and Kirk Laing's home to evaluate local Florence interest, breaking those off when Bob and Anne moved to Atlanta.

Rob Colones and Bob Hinshelwood went on to become key McLeod Hospital and Medical Center administrators, the Laings to become very successful entrepreneurs after a missionary stint in Italy, and Dr. Adams to build a prestigious obstetrics-gynecology surgical practice in Florence.

As the home studies grew and grew, even in the absence of Pastor Bob, the three founding couples realized it was time for more. They wanted to start an evangelical Christian church in Florence with an emphasis on evangelism, on Christian living with growth in Christian understanding and individual development, and on missions. In faith, the Norrises moved to Florence from Atlanta in 1986 at Rob Colones's request, thus founding the Heritage Church (Rob Colones became chairman of the elders), later to become the Church at Sandhurst in 1990. The new church had both a board of elders and a deacon board. The three founding couples all lived in or near the Heritage neighborhood in Florence, thus the name of the new church, the Heritage Church.

Church at Sandhurst

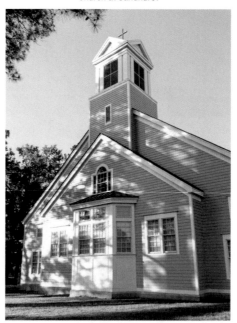

STEPHEN A. IMBEAU was born on November 25, 1947, in Portland, Oregon, growing up in Oakland, California. He attended college at the University of California, Berkeley, to study mathematics and computer science and then medical school at the University of California, San Francisco, graduating with a medical doctorate in May of 1973. He completed his internship and residency in internal medicine at the University of Wisconsin in 1977 and an allergy fellowship in June 1979. He married Shirley Ruth Burke of Toronto, Canada, in Toronto on August 18, 1979.

Shirley Ruth Burke was born on April 17, 1955, in Toronto, Ontario, as the only daughter and third child of four to John Donald Burke, born March 29, 1922, in Trenton, Ontario, and Frances Phyllis Clark, born March 16, 1921, in Toronto, Ontario. Mr. Burke never went past the sixth grade in school, but built a successful international silver plating and silver repair business called Burke and Wallace Limited, headquartered in Toronto. Shirley studied education at the University of Toronto. She graduated in 1977, taking a school teacher job at the Peel District School Board, working for almost two years at the Herb Campbell Public School and the Mayfield High School, before marrying and moving to Madison, Wisconsin.

Both Shirley and Steve grew up in what is called broadly the "Brethren" tradition, a conservative branch called "Closed Brethren" or "Renton Brethren" or "Plymouth Brethren." The Brethren were distinctive for dispensational theology, weekly services for the "Breaking of the Bread," and often without paid pastors, as well as many divisions over the years.

In February 1980, we left Wisconsin to come to Florence, arriving on March 1, 1980, to three inches of snow, joining Dr. Peter Williams's allergy practice; we have been in Florence ever since. The first five years or so were tumultuous; after a few twists and turns, I began my own allergy practice in

Florence as the first board-certified allergist in the region. The practice moved from independent practice to join the Carolina Health Care Group, then to the Pee Dee Internal Medicine Group, and then I and Dr. Joseph Moyer founded the Allergy, Asthma and Sinus Center in 1996.

Shirley and I joined the early Heritage neighborhood Bible studies in early 1985, invited by Rob Colones soon after he and I met through the emergency room at McLeod Hospital. Rob and I played racquetball together (with him always beating me), and one day I turned to him and said, "I have never heard you swear; are you a Christian?" And he responded, "Yes."

Shirley and I were then driving over to a small Columbia, South Carolina, Brethren house church, but were determined to attend Bob's first formal church service in Florence. We remember Pastor Bob's first Sunday in Florence in September 1986. The church met at the YMCA and Bob stood out on the front porch to make sure the guests found their way. There were thirteen people at that first service (the original three couples, the Imbeau couple, Munford Scott with three, and the Norrises). But Heritage Church grew and grew and grew, moving from a small YMCA board meeting room to the weight room and then to the gymnasium. Shirley and I continued on as visitors for about seven more years before officially joining.

Not long after that first Sunday visit, Deb Colones told Shirley she needed to borrow our warm coats for the Norrises

Florence YMCA entrance

Weight room

Church at Sandhurst entrance

to use as they traveled in winter to Canada for Bob's father's funeral. I was shocked when Shirley suggested a quality English lamb wool coat—I gave them a ski coat instead. We have laughed at my reluctance ever since. After about six months of visiting the church, one Sunday Pastor Bob invited me for lunch; my first thought was, "Oh, bother, what does he want?" Or "What have I done?" But he just wanted to eat and talk; I enjoyed it. I realized that he really wanted to be a friend, not just a pastor, and had an interest in me as an individual. I also had to work through my natural distaste for pastors, since Closed Brethren churches typically had no pastors. Bob and I soon met again and then later the four of us as couples; we bonded almost magically. The common non-Christian tie was that both Anne and Shirley were schoolteachers and Bob and Shirley both Canadians.

Bob and I began to visit every Tuesday night in about 1988 with the folks leaving behind Sunday morning church visitor cards. At first, there were about ten Heritage Church folks who volunteered to visit in pairs, rotating with the pastor; I was assigned to Bob Hinshelwood, Kirk Laing, and Della Powers, but we did not have compatible schedules, so I ended up with the pastor as one of the visiting pairs. Eventually, only we two carried on.

The Pattern

*"Let all things be done decently
and in order."* 1 CORINTHIANS 14:40

*"But we will give ourselves
continually to prayer, and to the
ministry of the word."* ACTS 6:4

*"Feed the flock of God which
is among you"* 1 PETER 5:2A

PASTOR BOB AND I developed a visiting pattern, a certain style. Tuesday nights were for the Church at Sandhurst visiting and we both arranged our schedules to make certain we were available each Tuesday night. Because of my travel schedule, we missed some nights, but not many, as most of my travel was Friday to Monday.

I would pick Bob up from his home at 7:00 p.m. during the summer and 6:30 p.m. otherwise. Bob would always lead in prayer on the drive before we embarked. We drove around Florence for about two hours maximum, seeing two to three couples. I was the driver and he the navigator. He had several Florence maps from gas stations and the tourist office. Finding remote addresses was sometimes a chore, as he would turn the maps this way and that way, to find the correct streets. He often would mark up the maps. Eventually, GPS made things a lot easier. Sometimes the visitor cards were hard to read and sometimes we just called the folks to ask for directions (but we avoided phone calls because we were often prematurely turned away). We found all the addresses, eventually, and learned the Florence geography better than ever intended.

Bob would organize the visitor cards ahead, usually choosing five (in case some folks were not home) trying to place them all in the same part of Florence. Some were folks he had already met, but most were new to us both (although often we ran into friends or patients–Florence being a small town). Typically, Bob had already visited some folks on his own or over one of his famous lunches. So, on Tuesday nights we visited folks who he couldn't otherwise reach or who worked during the day.

We tried to park discretely, on the street, between two addresses, and always careful to never ride over or park on lawns. We wanted to be prim and proper and so were also careful to stay out of driveways and never to block access. Apartment complex parking was sometimes difficult, but we didn't mind having to walk a bit.

We preferred door or screen door knocks, rather than doorbells, but used them sequentially, as needed; in the summer, we might walk to the backyard if we heard noise. We always dressed in business attire with coat and tie and smiled brightly as the door was opened. Bob would say, "I am Pastor Bob Norris of the Church at Sandhurst and this is Dr. Steve Imbeau. We are answering your offering plate visitor's card and would like to come in for a visit. Okay? Is this a good time?" Usually, we were invited in.

Rarely did we accept offers of food or drink, but for water or iced tea in the summer. We didn't want any implied obligations on either side. But once we did join a back porch chicken dinner, to be polite and because the man of the house told us, "You want to visit? Well, then sit down and join us." We did but really didn't eat much.

We tried to limit visits to thirty minutes and strove to visit three families per night. Although visiting as a pair with business dress, we avoided women alone, although broke that rule if they already knew one of us well. Three times we found newcomers to Florence on the phone with their husbands, and the ladies invited us in, saying that she and her husband were both believers, and he wanted to stay on the line and hear what we had to say. We did. All three of these couples became steadfast members of the Sandhurst Family and all three husbands became elders or deacons; the couples have since moved on, one to Tennessee (the Hardens), one to North Carolina (the Moores), and one to Texas (the Hoffarts).

Storms and rain were controversial. First of all, we didn't want to track mud or water into folks' homes, and sometimes storms bother both people and animals. But Bob, too, just didn't like the rain. At first, I would tease him unmercifully, "Bob, you mean the Holy Spirit doesn't like the rain, or he can't function in the rain?" or, "Bob, I thought you believed the Holy Spirit was inside you? Why, I have seen you swim at my house, and I am sure you take showers, so what is this about rain?" Eventually, I stopped the jokes as he *never* gave in. But we found something almost as good as visiting during storms: restaurant desserts. So, rainy Tuesday nights usually found us at The Florentine in the Huntington Plaza eating pie and talking; see, we can visit with each other, too—and having a grand old time bonding and becoming even better friends. Bob's favorite pie remains my secret.

The Norrises and the Imbeaus became friends even before the visiting. And so, to include our wives and bond as couples, once every three months or so, we four went out to dinner on a Tuesday evening, rather than church visiting. Bob and Anne loved going out for meals and knew all the best restaurants within a hundred-mile radius of Florence. In fact, they sort of had a restaurant ministry. They tried to rotate around Florence among their favorite places and made a special point of making friends among the waiters, cooks, and management. They came to know most by first name and even went to some homes as quests for meals. Many restaurant folks came to Jesus or were comforted or counseled through this Norris casual mini-ministry. Thus, Bob and Anne were our dinner experts: in Florence—The Florentine, Victors, the Grotto, PA's, the Oasis, Thai II, Anne's Thai Kitchen, Da Massimo; in Camden–Lilfred's; in Myrtle Beach—Gulfstream Café, Angelo's, the Bistro; and occasionally even to Fayetteville. Sometimes they also forced me to buy new clothes at their favorite clothiers in Florence, Sumter, and Columbia; I usually don't like shopping for clothes. We would review our lives, give updates on the family, and eventually plan some trips.

Starting in 1993, we began to take some trips together as two couples, sometimes to visit remote Sandhurst missionaries. We had a certain travel rhythm: mornings free or for talk and Bible readings and prayer; then touring and lunch; then more touring, with some free time in the afternoon before dinner and usually a quiet night; every third day was a free day away from each other. Since often built around medical meetings, Steve was often off to study and learn. We rarely fought or even had disputes; well, there was one time on a train in Italy. Shirley and Anne usually picked the day's schedule, Bob carried the maps and directed us, and Steve provided the history. Bob usually did the driving. The trips were usually to an Allergy or Asthma meeting and always with our green carry-on bag. The green bag became famous over the years, and when damaged in a car accident was preserved as an important souvenir.

Our visitation built up Sandhurst. For a time, two to three couples per month became new Christians and usually ended up joining the Sandhurst family. We never counted the numbers, but at its peak, about three years before Bob left, the family was up to about nine hundred adults.

"And You Say . . . ?"

*"Whom do men say that I the Son of man am? . . .
But whom say ye that I am?"* MATTHEW 16:13B,15B

*"I say unto you, that likewise joy
shall be in heaven over one sinner
that repenteth."* LUKE 15:7A

*"That if thou shalt confess with thy mouth
the Lord Jesus, and shalt believe in thine
heart that God hath raised him from the
dead, thou shalt be saved."* ROMANS 10:9

WE WERE NOT ONLY VISITORS but evangelists, hopefully with a gentle touch. Once inside the home with a family or couple, Bob would usually have me break the ice with some local social chit-chat and then Bob would lean in with a story: "So, let's say you all and I are driving with Steve here, going to get some bread and milk, and we have an accident at the corner, an eighteen-wheeler careening into us, sending us all to the gates of heaven. Saint Peter stands and asks, 'Why should I let you into God's heaven?' And you say . . . ?"

When Bob asked, "And you say . . . ?" we got both expected and surprising responses from folks. Since they had filled out visitor cards marked "I want a visit from the pastor" or at least "Interested," these were all folks interested in the church. At least we so assumed.

The most amusing response was the one just after we knocked or rang the doorbell; the "I really don't want to see you" response. Some people are very inventive. We have had all of the following shouted at us from behind windows, through windows, from behind backyard fences, and from behind front doors:

- "Nobody home!" (*Huh, who just yelled at us, then, a burglar or a lost cousin?*)
- "Not interested." (*But we have a card from Sandhurst here that says "Interested."*)
- "We're on the way out." (*Well, when can we come back?*)
- "I just got out of the shower." (Actually, this one more times than you would expect.)
- "I'm getting dressed." (*Okay . . . ? We'll wait.* But, then usually an opened door and an embarrassed brush off.)
- "It wasn't me." (*Okay, can we come back later to see . . .* reading the name on the card.)
- "I've changed my mind." (Okay, hard to argue with that.)

The other 90 percent of responses were to invite us in, seated, usually mostly comfortably, but occasionally we were still standing at an open door or draped over lawn or patio furniture.

I always inwardly groaned at the, "Before I answer you, I've got a few questions," response because it usually meant a long visit, or sometimes, the only visit for that night. Remember, the Luther–Erasmus debates went on for years; the Council of Trent took at least seven years. The questions were usually aimed at the church's statement of faith, or something Bob had preached the Sunday they had come, or something that was a "bone in the craw" of this person, or someone just trying to find out about our personal or church politics or to push their brand of humor.

The statement of faith or sermon issues could usually be turned around to some quotes or readings from Scripture or some sort of biblical or gospel presentation. But the "bone in the craw" thing was often tough when we let the visitee turn the tables on us. You can probably predict: "They say this, what say you?" "I grew up _____ and your statement of faith contradicts what I was taught." On more than one night we endured lectures on:

- TULIP, characterizing John Calvin's assumed theology. (How could we break in and say we agree with some but not all?)
- "What do you think about angels?" (We got this question much more than I expected.)
- "Where is God?"
- "Why has such and such happened to me?" And onwards to the biggy:
- "What do you all think about Prophecy?"

We were patient and hoped to leave gently. Only occasionally did we ever see these questioning folks again, as they just never came back to Sandhurst. We can only apologize.

Even in the Bible Belt South, about 10 percent of the time we heard: "Certainly I'm not coming in here, not to heaven" or "I can't come in, I'm going straight to hell," usually with a shrug or some sort of laugh. Well, we never batted an eye but launched into a response with several avenues of approach. "Why do you say that?" or, "Is that the way you want it?" or, "Do

you want to know the way to heaven?" in order to preach at
least a little gospel.

About 30 percent of the time we had bright smiles all
around and affirmation of Christian faith, with, "Of course, I
am a Christian," or, "I know Jesus as my Savior," or, "I accepted
Christ at age _____ ," or, "I so much am looking forward to being
with my Lord and Savior." Even then, as the pastor and mentor,
Bob probed further. "Tell me about your salvation experience
(or conversion or testimony)." And then would follow their
life stories and how they became Christians. Often, too, Bob
would then share the story of his youth and how his grandmother helped to lead him to the Lord; and then the story of
Anne Russell. And sometimes me, about my early childhood
conversion; my later careless lifestyle in college and medical
school; my unusual meeting of Shirley in August of 1978 at a
Brethren conference (through her cousin Patsy Harlow, coming out of what I thought was a coincidental June 1978 dinner
in Chicago), and then the delayed dinner appointment in late
June 1978 with my sister and friends in Santa Cruz, California,
forcing me to confront the possibility that the Lord's Second
Coming had been accomplished and that I was "left behind."

And then Bob would ask if they had any questions about
Sandhurst, starting off with his number one point: member-
ship at Sandhurst depended on "knowing that you know that
Jesus is your personal Savior." With subsequent review of the
statement of faith, the church's programs, and schedules. And
of course, time for questions, sometimes lots of questions.

A few folks would answer, "I want to be in heaven, but I am
not sure how to answer Saint Peter. Can you help me?" Well,
here was an obvious opportunity for a simple Christian gospel
message if you ever saw one, and we never avoided it. But uncertainty was the response from the largest group of couples.

Uncertainty and Venn Diagrams

"For God so loved the world, that he gave his only begotten Son, that whosoever believeth in him should not perish, but have everlasting life." JOHN 3:16

"When Aquila and Priscilla had heard, they took him unto them, and expounded unto him the way of God more perfectly." ACTS 18:26

AND SO, "And you say . . . ?"

When Bob asked this question, uncertainty was the response from the largest group of our hosts. At least one would answer, "I don't know," or, "I hope I can enter in," or, "I was baptized," or, "I was confirmed," or, "I go to church each Sunday," or, "I think I'm a Christian." And here was a great opportunity for Bob.

To these uncertain folks, he would sit back and smile—he has a delightful smile, makes me jealous—and since most of our couples were married, he would usually inquire, "How do you know you're married?" Then he would go on to explain about knowing you are married, not guessing at it, or that there is no such thing as a partial marriage. In other words, you are either married or not, not somewhere in between. There is no uncertainty. Well, you see Christianity can be like that, without uncertainty.

Then a brief gospel: first, the story of the nativity, Jesus's birth in Bethlehem, and then his early years. His bar mitzvah and then his years of ministry around Palestine after being anointed by the Holy Spirit at John the Baptist's hands at age thirty. Then his miracles and the other evidence he was the Son of God. Then his last days, the Hebrew trial, the Roman trial, and the Roman crucifixion. And then his resurrection. And then Paul's testimony and ringing gospel from the books of Acts and Romans. Romans 5:8–9 says, "But God commendeth his love toward us, in that, while we were yet sinners, Christ died for us. Much more then, being now justified by his blood, we shall be saved from wrath through him." Then Bob would explain that God punished Jesus for your sins, my sins, all of our sins for all time, past and future, and Jesus's resurrection proves the acceptance of God's sacrifice of his Son so that now you can have eternal life and forgiveness of sins through him. The Christian gospel was simply told in home after home in about ten or fifteen minutes over almost twenty-five years of Tuesday nights.

Then, after a pause or a sip of water: "Do you follow this story? Do you believe it? What is keeping you from becoming a Christian right now, tonight, right here? Can you think of anything preventing you tonight? Tell me what it is and we can explore it together. Do you accept Jesus?"

And then the Venn diagrams. (I doubt if Bob knows much about John Venn and his mathematics from 1880.) He used them as circles representing in the outside circle, the whole of humanity, with two inner circles: one for all people professing or hoping to be Christians, another of "true" Christians (Christians who know they know Jesus as personal savior) with the overlap of the two inner circles. He would ask our listeners to point to where they would fall in the three circles that he drew out on a handy paper napkin or piece of stationery. Were they in the outer circle (non-Christian)? Were they in the hopeful Christian circle (unsure)? Or were they in the other believing circle (assured)? Would they now move themselves into the believing (or assurance) circle?

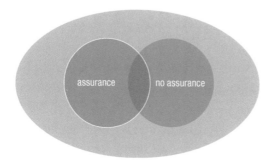

Preaching the gospel with Venn Diagrams

Bob wanted to make sure that all the unsure, if they knew Jesus as personal savior, also knew that they could have the certain assurance of Christian salvation. He wanted them to move from the inner two-circle "overlap" into the assurance circle alone. In other words, a Christian believer is by rights an assured Christian. Bob called this profound assurance "the assurance of salvation" and sometimes quoted from applicable scriptures, mostly in John's books. 1 John 5:13 says, "These things have I written unto you that believe on the name of the Son of God; that ye may know that ye have eternal life, and that ye may believe on the name of the Son of God." And John 1:12 says, "But as many as received him, to them gave he power to become the sons of God, even to them that believe on his name."

We wanted to emphasize over and over not only the Christian gospel but also that Christianity comes with assurance and that its reliability can be counted on, taken as a surety. No longer does a Christian believer need to say, "I think so," nor, "I hope so." With the assurance of Christian salvation comes thus the peace and joy of salvation.

Bob would often demonstrate assurance by standing and then sitting heavily on a chair or couch, saying, "I will let my whole weight down on this furniture; that means I am certain about it, I trust it, and I believe in it. This is the point I am making; my reliance on the couch demonstrates complete faith and assurance." But in one home, even though he asked ahead, the piano bench he picked for his assurance demonstration collapsed, and he fell right down to the floor, no harm done. Imagine his surprise and the near panic of our hosts, but all was OK. After he picked himself up without harm, we all laughed. Those folks will never forget that demonstration of "assurance."

Partnership

*"Thou art my hiding place; thou shalt
preserve me from trouble; thou
shalt compass me about with songs
of deliverance."* PSALM 32:7

*"Yea, though I walk through
the valley of the shadow of death,
I will fear no evil: for thou art
with me; thy rod and thy staff,
they comfort me."* PSALM 23:4A

*"Every purpose is established by
counsel."* PROVERBS 20:18A

TWENTY-FIVE YEARS is a long time. A whole generation. Bob Norris and I visited together for the Church at Sandhurst for twenty-five years. The end came in 2013 with no great, finalizing event or crisis, no fanfare, and no cataclysm. It was just time to stop. Anne saw the end coming first, watching Bob closely and protectively. Besides, Sandhurst was already looking around for a new pastor with Bob's assistance. We two couples quietly honored the visiting termination with a dinner out at Da Massimo, then in Hartsville, to review the visiting years; so many memories and so many trips together. We still stay in touch and still enjoy our special dinners, usually out, but sometimes now at our home. The deep friendship endures.

Bob and I spent a lot of time together on Tuesday nights. Just driving around, we had time to talk and visit with each other, not to mention our rainy night dessert times. We talked about family, some church dilemmas, and his job as chair of Columbia Bible College and Seminary/Columbia International University (during most of the presidential tenure of Dr. George Murray). Family, particularly, held our attention. And sometimes planning our next trip.

Columbia International University entrance

Bob's family was mostly grown and in college, mine just beginning (Stephanie, our first child, was born in 1982, and Charles, our last, was born in 1989). But we had plenty of troubles to discuss and to lean towards each other, mostly over our boys. Growing pains, adjustments in school, dating troubles, school troubles, job troubles, and then marriage troubles. So much happened within our families over those twenty-five years. All these struggles kept us both humble and accountable to each other and often found us ending the evening in Bob's driveway deep in prayer, sometimes hugging each other, sometimes even with tears in our eyes.

We both would both immediately respond to any family emergency, driving to the other's home. I will never forget how

Bob came to Shirley's side to spend overnight hours, sleeping in a chair, in her time of need after Charles's birth, how he came to see Andrew in an emergency, and then how he came for Charles. Bob was close to us as we began to realize that our dear, and oh, so smart Charles had come down with a chronic illness and that Shirley had come down with cancer. Bob was our pastor, yes, but these and other circumstances brought out more, true love and the fruit of our hours together. I never will forget the difficult but special times that we ended Tuesday visiting early in order to spend time together discussing and praying for our children.

Bob would sometimes ask me to pray with him about some important, specific issue of current concern at the Church at Sandhurst. He was careful to never talk about elder nor deacon meetings, and I never asked. I was never much involved in Sandhurst governance. I was outside the church governance partly because personnel management is not "my thing," partly because of my travel schedules, partly because of my personality, and partly because of my involvement in the secular world. But I understood and knew "all this." We feel part of Sandhurst, even so, and Shirley and I maintained our presence at Sandhurst, even after Bob retired and moved over to the Church at King Avenue. We continue to view Sandhurst as our church home.

But I was quietly involved behind the scenes in several key issues along the way, partly at Bob's request, but also with the concurrence of the church elders. In these four issues (six individuals involved; sadly, three were Sandhurst teachers or leaders), the strategy was to first get me, and often others, involved as a thoughtful, but forceful, counter, and then for the elders to deal with the individual people. Ironically, one of the early issues was eternal security, given the thrust of so much of our church visiting and our emphasis on the assurance of salvation. One day, a prominent member started to dominate one of the Sunday school classes with questions about "losing your salvation" and how he had been restored and saved again, in fact, "walking down the aisle" over and over.

To counter gracefully, the Sunday school teacher, Chip Register, started a series on eternal security; my job was to challenge the class with questions or comments, usually gently, and to read or quote from the Bible supporting eternal security. As you might expect, we often referred to 1 John 5:13, "These things have I written unto you that believe on the name of the Son of God; that ye may know that ye have eternal life, and that ye may believe on the name of the Son of God." And John 10:27–28: "My sheep hear my voice, and I know them, and they follow me: and I give unto them eternal life; and they shall never perish, neither shall any man pluck them out of my hand." And John 3:16: "For God so loved the world, that he gave his only begotten Son, that whosoever believeth in him should not perish, but have everlasting life." Both everlasting life and eternal life mean just that, life in Christ forever for the believer, no matter what else comes later in life.

The second issue is loosely called "mysticism," which is not much different from ancient "Gnosticism." The idea that there is either some secret Christian knowledge that only the most pious or holy or the attuned can attain, or that some Christians have special "spirit" or powers goes way back and, of course, has become mainstream in some Christian denominations. But Christianity is not mystical. In fact, Paul uses the word "to know" or "knowledge" or the phrase "use your brain (mind)" up to a hundred times in his biblical epistles. Paul urges sober thinking and behavior for Christians, not trances, chants, unknown language, or drug enhancements for worship and appreciation of God. For reasons unknown to me, the mysticism mostly came up in prayers at the Sandhurst "Breaking of

Bread" (what some traditions call "Communion" or "the Lord's table" or "the Lord's Supper" or "the Eucharist" or "Mass").

My mission was to stand up in the service and read aloud from Scripture without comment, usually from biblical passages arguing against mysticism. Here are my favorite passages, chosen according to the circumstance:

> "For I am persuaded, that neither death, nor life,
> nor angels, nor principalities, nor powers, nor things
> present, nor things to come, nor height, nor depth,
> nor any other creature, shall be able to separate us
> from the love of God, which is in Christ Jesus our
> Lord." (ROMANS 8:38–39)

> "Forasmuch as ye know that ye were not redeemed
> with corruptible things, as silver and gold, from your
> vain conversation received by tradition from your
> fathers; but with the precious blood of Christ, as of a
> lamb without blemish and without spot." (I PETER 1:18–19)

> "Now to him that is of power to stablish you
> according to my gospel, and the preaching of Jesus
> Christ, according to the revelation of the mystery,
> which was kept secret since the world began, but
> now is made manifest, and by the Scriptures of
> the prophets, according to the commandment of
> the everlasting God, made known to all nations for
> the obedience of faith: to God only wise, be glory
> through Jesus Christ for ever. Amen." (ROMANS 16:25–27)

> "That Christ may dwell in your hearts by faith; that
> ye, being rooted and grounded in love, may be able
> to comprehend with all saints what is the breadth,
> and length, and depth, and height; and to know
> the love of Christ, which passeth knowledge, that
> ye might be filled with all the fulness of God. Now
> unto him that is able to do exceeding abundantly

above all that we ask or think, according to the
power that worketh in us, unto him be glory in
the church by Christ Jesus throughout all ages,
world without end. Amen." (EPHESIANS 3:17–21)

"But we see Jesus, who was made a little lower
than the angels for the suffering of death, crowned
with glory and honour; that he by the grace of God
should taste death for every man." (HEBREWS 2:9)

"Now the God of peace, that brought again from
the dead our Lord Jesus, that great shepherd of the
sheep, through the blood of the everlasting covenant,
make you perfect in every good work to do his
will, working in you that which is wellpleasing
in his sight, through Jesus Christ; to whom be
glory for ever and ever. Amen." (HEBREWS 13:20–21)

And often my favorite:

"For God so loved the world, that he gave his only
begotten Son, that whosoever believeth in him should
not perish, but have everlasting life." (JOHN 3:16)

You see, the simple counter to mysticism is Jesus Christ
himself, who as both human and God, with his death and
resurrection as God's self-sacrifice for sin expedites for those
who believe, who accept, salvation and eternal life. You can
depend on it, you can know it. It is not mystical because he is
the Man, Christ Jesus. His history, sacrifice, resurrection, and
assumption are all well recorded and verified.

The third issue was what we call "universalism" or the notion that since we are all God's creation, eventually we all will
come to him and salvation even if not through Jesus Christ,
which is contrary to what we have outlined in previous

chapters. Universalism also often mixes in strange theology about Jesus and whether he is really God or not, or when he became God (a kind of ancient Arianism). There are basically two tenets intertwined: one, that since we are all created in God's image and given that God is love, somehow we will all end up in his eternal spiritual family no matter the life or behavior path we are on—he will find us; and two, that this path, this relationship that God finds or wants for us, need not be through Jesus or his sacrifice for sin on the literal cross two thousand years ago. This heretical notion is prevalent among many TV preachers, novelists, and Hollywood. Well, it started to spread around Sandhurst, too, particularly after the publication of the novel, *The Shack*, which is basically a Universalist manifesto, engagingly written and a smash best seller with a movie to boot. Unfortunately, a large group of folks left Sandhurst over this issue, although some have since returned. I was asked to write an essay about the novel and Rob Colones also did independent research into the novel and its author excerpting a review by Tim Challies.

Focusing on *The Shack*, we were struck by the lack of any scriptural reference. You would expect a Christian book that includes dialog with the Trinity and Wisdom to use some scriptures, particularly since the biblical Jesus quoted from the Old Testament all the time. It's out of character for neither God, Jesus, nor the Holy Spirit to quote from Hebrew Scripture. You would also expect the Trinity, if speaking to us in our modern era, to affirm their own biblical New Testament apostles and disciples' writings, historic influence, and establishment of the early Christian church. Quite frankly, the lack of any biblical reference or quotes makes the novel's theology suspect on the surface, even before analysis.

But what the characters portraying the Trinity in *The Shack* actually do say is also quite egregious and erroneous. There is no acknowledgment of sin nor requirement for a sin sacrifice or sin atonement; rather the speakers say they come to people through relationship, through a process, through a conversation, by developing a relationship, by making themselves open to people. There is no sense in the novel of the uniqueness of salvation through Jesus, no concept that there is no way to God but through Jesus, (i.e., "I am the way, the truth, and the life: no man cometh unto the Father, but by me," John 14:6; also see Romans 3–5), and certainly no idea of required blood sacrifice or the death of Jesus. In fact, just the opposite. The book's characters say, "I have no desire to make people Christians, but I do want to join them in their transformation into sons and daughters of God, into brothers and sisters, into My Beloved." Such psychobabble and rhetoric, even if soaring, may make you feel good, it even may make you feel noble and secure, particularly if sin guilt is removed, but it is not the biblical way to God. Remember, we humans are not gods, we cannot come to God on our own, we cannot create our own nirvana or our own heaven. If we reject the way of the cross, if we reject the blood sacrifice of Jesus Christ as the only way to salvation from sin, then we have rejected God's only plan of salvation.

In fact, God *does* love all his human creation, he *is* universal, and so he provided, at great, infinite cost, his Son as the propitiation for all sin and all people. Jesus died because God *is* love. For remember, "For God so loved the World, that he gave his only begotten Son, that whosoever believeth in him should not perish, but have everlasting life." But also remember that at the marriage feast in Jesus's parable, the groom's father was well pleased to have all kinds of folks at the wedding including the worse sinners of all types and including folks that knew nothing about him nor his son, *but* he expected all to wear the wedding clothes he provided at the door (Matthew 22).

The final issue was mostly Bob's concern. The church and the elders were long split and therefore usually quiet about the non-essential general interpretation of the Bible into more or less two distinct, but actually blurred, camps of covenantal theology and dispensational theology. Bob distributed a book on the topic to the elders and anybody else who wanted one. Bob's upcoming retirement, some of the personal philosophies of his potential replacement pastors, one major donor family, and a rising star divinity school student brought the issue to a head. But all was quietly resolved, and the church continues as before, tilting towards dispensationalism, but really quietly split between the two theologies.

This outcome I personally view as positive. The two theologies basically split over the place or the role of the Hebrew people in God's will or plan for both the time after Christ's earthly life and during or after his second return; these points about the Hebrew peoples correlate with the future role of the Christian church. The questions can be framed as, "Can both the Hebrews and the Christians be God's chosen people or does Christianity replace Judaism?" or, "Is salvation in the Old Testament different than salvation in the New Testament?" or, "Do the Old Testament promises or covenants apply to the Hebrew people in the modern or future eras or are they transferred to the Christian church?" and, "Is God's earthly millennial kingdom literal with Jesus as King or is it the fully sanctified Christian church that governs?"

While there are some fine point disagreements internal to both theologies, the dispensationalist believes that God deals with man through history in a series of dispensations— innocence, independence or conscience, human government, God-authored law, grace, holy kingship (the government during the Millennium depicted in John's biblical Revelation), and the eternal state. The dispensationalist views man as a *failure* under each of them (including the age of grace or the church age and even the theocracy)—except for the last age.

The covenantalist views God's dealing with man through covenant: the Adamic covenant, the Abrahamic covenant, the Mosaic covenant, the Davidic covenant, the covenant of grace, and the new covenant (John Calvin listed seven covenants but includes two under Abraham and some writers also include a covenant of Noah). The covenantalist views the Christian church in the last five covenants and *not* as failed, but instead as eventually triumphant. The covenantalist believes that, since the time of Abraham, Israel was the focus of the early covenants, but failed and was divorced from God as portrayed in Ezekiel, and after Jesus's assumption, was replaced by the Christian church which in the power of the new covenant shall eventually reign over the earth for at least a thousand years. The covenantalist believes that any gospel or prophecy of Jesus is intertwined with Judaism and that thus Christianity and Judaism should be viewed in unity, whether preached in the Old Testament or the New Testament. Both theologies have support in the Bible depending on the passages and the interpretations.

Traditional historic Christianity is covenantal, although Augustine (360) provides some basis to the modern dispensationalists; Jerome (360) resisted Augustine and, eventually, Thomas Aquinas (1250) moved the Roman Catholic Church, along with the Eastern Church, to retreat from the Augustinian position on Israel. The Westminster Confession (1646) is the bedrock document of protestant covenantal theology. The modern dispensational theology springs from the writings and teachings of John Nelson Darby (1830 onwards), first proposed and explored at the Powerscourt Conferences (1832) and then promoted and popularized in the United States by D. L. Moody, Cyrus Schofield, and the Dallas Seminary. For some history and commentary, see T. B. Baines, *The Lord's Coming: Israel and the Church*. But it is important that these two theologies have *no* impact on the bedrock Christian theologies of the Trinity; the creation; original sin; the divinity of Jesus; the bodily, bloody sacrificial triumph of Jesus over sin, death, and hell; the assumption of Jesus; the work of the Holy Spirit; nor the future glory of Jesus and the church universal in heaven and eternity.

The essential doctrines of Christianity are not affected by the two theologies. And thus the two theologies should not be allowed to divide Christians. But they can divide, and they do divide. For modern context, note the enduring major differences, even with historic conflict and persecution, between the Reformed and Presbyterian Protestant church against the Baptist Church and the much smaller, declining Brethren Assemblies. Among all Protestants, the covenantalists outnumber the dispensationalists.

Theological supremacy or control often leads to smugness and arrogance. We can be legalistic and arrogant about our Christian convictions or preferences, even ones not requisite for salvation. So, thus I say that a quiet disagreement among the leadership of the Church at Sandhurst over covenantal versus dispensational theology is a good thing. "Be of good cheer; love one another."

I was proud of Bob's chairmanship at Columbia International University in Columbia, South Carolina. He is the longest-serving member on the CIU Board, serving from February 1974 to May 2013 both before and after his chairmanship. He was a loyal board member and supporter of CIU. He loved to attend the CIU Chapel and preach or teach when asked. He rarely missed the two to three day quarterly board meetings, and, of course, had to go to Columbia even more often when he was the chair. But he rarely if ever mentioned this work from the Sandhurst pulpit, and since I was not from a denominational background, I would have never known either, but for our Tuesday visits. We often prayed for some normal CIU institutional and spiritual problems. Occasionally, knowing I had "big world" experience, he would ask me about a specific circumstance where he thought I could give advice. He brought many CIU folks over to teach or preach at Sandhurst, particularly Dr. Jack Layman and Dr. Terry Hulbert. Both befriended Shirley and me, shared many meals with us, and occasionally stayed overnight in our home.

Stories Along the Way:
The People

"And God Almighty bless thee, and make
thee fruitful, and multiply thee, that thou
mayest be a multitude of people." GENESIS 28:3

"I have considered the days of old, the
years of ancient times. I call to remembrance
my song in the night." PSALM 77:5–6A

"The cloke that I left at Troas with
Carpus, when thou comest, bring with
thee, and the books, but especially
the parchments." 2 TIMOTHY 4:13

SO MANY YEARS and so many stories. One couple at a time, Tuesday night after Tuesday night, we saw lots of people in all sorts of situations. We saw great diversity: all walks of life, all professions, all economic status, all spiritual backgrounds, and all races. We saw it all. Good thing we both loved people and being with people and such stories. Some individuals just stood out or made a special impact on us that night, or later on at the church. But of course, there are similarities among peoples, so that many stories are really group stories, as similar scenarios often do occur over and over, albeit with different individuals.

We have already written about the influence of several women in the church, their intent to come and join, and their influence on their husbands to move into leadership roles. And we also watched important hospitality, not only to us visitors but to the whole church. The family dinners, often including non-family, of the Sims (both family sets), the Laings, the Wilsons, the Jacksons, the Stuckeys, the Johnsons, the Hultgrens, the Adams, and several other families became famous and important in building the body of Christ at Sandhurst, member by member, meal by meal, often on Sunday afternoons.

I first met Tommy Head in a Lynches River flood. I have never forgotten him. He was perched atop his back porch with a wine bottle, his favorite pickle jar, a grand smile, and flowing hair, watching the river rise up his steps as we approached his porch from the street side. Bob already knew Tommy from the Church at Sandhurst baseball team. Despite a secular and reckless lifestyle, Tommy maintained a close friendship with Michael Wilson, a Sandhurst member, who invited Tommy to play softball with the Sandhurst team. The two had played AA professional baseball together.

Not long after our visit, Tommy began to come to Sandhurst almost every Sunday. And one Sunday afternoon, mowing his lawn, convicted by that day's sermon, he accepted Jesus as his savior. Angela had already come to Christ as a twelve-year-old child at the Treasure Island camp in Lynchburg, Virginia; but she had become wild and careless and rededicated her life after Tommy's conversion.

Tommy had an amazing mind, and even though he was not college educated, he held his own with the La-Z-Boy executives as he became a well-respected plant manager. He wanted to read more; he took speed-reading courses and memory retention courses. He read the Bible cover to cover many times and began to memorize it, not verse by verse, but chapter by chapter.

Unexpectedly, he and Angela went off to Peru to work with Amazon Focus. After a year of learning Spanish in Arequipa, they continued through the Andes to Pucallpa, a major city at the confluence of several rivers in the Peruvian Amazon jungle. There Tommy began to work with Amazon Focus, teaching at conferences for local churches and church leaders and in individual churches by invitation, both national and indigenous. Angela worked as a nurse and health instructor. They befriended folks at SAMAIR (South American Mission Aviation) and the Swiss Indian Mission stationed in Pucallpa. Often SAMAIR would fly them to the jungle conferences. The Heads built a home and later a guest cottage behind the SAMAIR station, on about five acres of land purchased from the Swiss Mission.

Eventually, Tommy and Angela, after working with several Amazon tribal groups, realized that clean water was a key jungle need. Rainwater and river water quickly became contaminated and thus damaging. Only well water could bring clean water. And so, they became well diggers, medical helpers, and missionary preachers across the Peruvian Amazon. This transition took them to Living Water International rather than Amazon Focus; they also worked with PLUS Oil and the Peruvian government. In order to provide even more funding for the well work, Tommy and his assistant, Jorge Antonio Álvarez Dávila, developed a small, successful real estate and construction business in Pucallpa. For a time they even worked with the World Wild Life Fund when the Fund was willing to help finance jungle village wells.

Tommy and Angela also helped to build up the Mil Palmeras Church in Pucallpa; Tommy and Julio Chiang were rotating preachers at the church with Julio the lead pastor. Julio was a well-known Peruvian champion motocross cyclist coming to the Lord through his mother and some evangelists.

Tommy and Julio developed a local motocross track that brought in some national races with national sponsors. Tommy loved the motocross track and rode as often as he could. He and Julio also developed a cadre of local motorcycle enthusiasts, planning cross-country trips into the Andes or into the jungle or just to ride. They often would cycle for several days staying in inns along the way or building their own campsites. Once, I joined Tommy for a day trip, riding one of his several motorcycles. An amusing story on this trip: we came across a police roadblock (a common way the local cops supplemented their incomes) asking for money; well, Tommy just shot ahead leaving me at the block, so I, acting like a typical American tourist, knowing no Spanish, shot after him, hoping to escape a shot in the back. About an hour later, we stopped at a roadside stand, and in walked the same police; they recognized us and just laughed and waived.

One tragic afternoon, about three months after my last visit to Pucallpa, Tommy, rushing along the motocross track more aggressively than usual, literally flying through the air with a grand smile on his face, landed poorly off a mogul, snapping his neck. He died instantly with the smile still on his face. He is buried on the site of his Peruvian cottage. Memorial services were held in Pucallpa and a couple of weeks later in Florence. People came from all over to overflowing fields and halls to remember and mourn and to hear poignant but joyful eulogies from Miguel Maturo, Wick Jackson (Wick spoke at both services), Greg Stuckey, and others.

Tommy died on April 25, 2009. Angela continued the well drilling work with Jorge for about six more years, before moving back to Florence to care for her parents.

We first visited John Gibson one late summer evening on his tractor, mowing his backyard. He was shirtless, dripping with sweat. But, on seeing us come up his driveway, he stopped mowing and told us he would shower fast. Within minutes, we were in his front room and with Pam, his cheerful wife with an endearing UK accent. They had met in England during John's military tour and later married. John was an accountant at DuPont and she a schoolteacher.

The Gibsons were Christians closely attached with a leadership role to Calvary Baptist Church, but they were attracted to the style of Sandhurst, its aura of personal freedom framed within orthodoxy. Hurricane Hugo was soon upon us, and even though not yet part of Sandhurst, John visited many of us cutting down obstructing trees (Bob's street was probably struck by a mini-tornado, too) and freeing up driveways. I called John "our angel."

Eventually, the Gibsons became part of the Sandhurst family, with John moving into leadership. In retirement, John worked with the church's missionary effort as bookkeeper and helper, including Wick Jackson's local business, for a time. Eventually, he became an elder at the little Church at King Avenue, when Pastor Bob officiated at both. It was a great loss when he and Pam moved to Columbia and Myrtle Beach to be with their grandchildren, his daughter Beth becoming a prominent accountant in South Carolina and a successful entrepreneur with Bauknight Pietras and Stormer. Beth was willing to provide "golden years" assistance to her parents.

Missionaries Paul (Paulo or Pablo or Pablito) and Robin Johnson moved to Florence in 1995 partly to be about half-way between Ontario, Canada, and Orlando, Florida, partly because they had started to work with the Sandhurst Missionary team headed by Dr. Steve Adams, and partly for rest and restoration. This Florence season proved to be a turning point in their lives. Sandhurst became a blessed springboard of restoration and strengthening, which launched them into one of the most visionary and productive chapters in their lives.

But we really did not meet them visiting, as they already knew Bob. Marrying in 1971 Paul and Robin had been working with World Outreach Fellowship and Sprint Missions to enable Amazon tribal contacts. From Harmony Church in Sumter, Jeff Norris, Bob's son, had done a trip with them in the Amazon, and Paul had also spoken at Harmony.

The Johnsons later transitioned to a work base in Orlando, Florida, and then moved to Florence. But we did visit them and eventually they rented a small house. They became an important part of the Sandhurst family, speaking and also hosting for about ten years the "Newly Marrieds" class, first at the Jackson home and then at the church site.

Paul spoke frequently at Sandhurst and was a regular part of the February Missions Conference for about 10 years. One Missions Conference appearance was particularly noteworthy. Paul entered the Sandhurst activity hall dressed as an Amazonian tribesman, in total disguise, speaking a native language. On his way to the platform, he stopped to marvel at Pastor Bob's mostly bald head, as baldness was unknown in his tribe. He then sat down around the campfire on stage to hear what the white missionaries had to say, as they tried to introduce him to the Gospel. Later, Steve Adams announced, "He also knows English." Lo and behold, it was Paul Johnson, to the surprise and delight of the audience.

Paul was an earnest missionary, living in South America since about age 8 when his parents left London, Ontario for the Bolivian jungle. He speaks multiple languages and can also speak with the animals, a useful skill when hunting or staying out of trouble in the jungle. He helped organize indigenous peoples, who became key partners with others, in sharing the Gospel with "unreached jungle peoples." Paul's gifts are in languages, preaching and teaching, organization, writing and fund raising (almost like a "one-man band.") Robin is always the quiet counselor and business manager. The entities the Johnsons created had several names, the most enduring being Amazon Focus and ALTECO. The Johnson's also founded Envoy International in 1995, now managed by Wick Jackson, also from Florence, South Carolina, and an Elder at the Church at Sandhurst. The Johnson's work took them to Pucallpa where they had a local partner and associate, Irma Espinoza. Tommy and Angela Head also lived in Pucallpa, originally serving with Amazon Focus. Years later, Tommy and Angela went on to work more closely with the Swiss Indian Mission, SAM Air, Living Water and the Mil Palmeras Church.

Paul had been a soccer star in South America and his athleticism and soccer skills were passed on to his sons. While at the Wesleyan College in South Carolina, Paul twice led the US, once in scoring and once in assists. He also went on to professional soccer, playing for the Litoral club in Bolivia and the London City club in Canada.

Paul has stepped back from day-to-day leadership in his mission initiatives to "open up space" for younger leaders. Presently he serves as a Strategic Consultant for ALTECO and the South America movement. He also takes time to write and speak at conferences in South America and churches in North America. The Johnsons are concentrating on developing a Communications website, on which they will upload challenging and informative mission information, particularly about the Amazon Region. This site will hold "Trilogies," comprised of songs or poems Paul has written over the years. The "birth stories" of each of these will be added, along with a challenge or summons applicable to each story. They're also developing a series of books about how God worked miraculously, through their life stories, jungle experiences, and mission endeavors. The Johnsons continue in the Sandhurst family.

The Imbeaus and the Johnsons eat Chinese together about every other month.

Once the Heads were Christians and part of Sandhurst, their good friends Carol and Henry (Andy) Anderson came, too, to "check it out" and see what Tommy was up to. The Andersons never expected to see the Heads in an evangelical Christian church. So, we visited the Andersons one Tuesday evening. They were mostly welcoming and certainly very casual. They listened politely to Bob's explanation of the gospel and Andy played some music for us. Carol was a well-respected local echocardiographer and had met Angela through the Bruce Hospital System; Andy was a handyman and commercial knife sharpener. He played music at local restaurants with a large following at Red Bone Alley. But Andy's interest in Christianity was piqued particularly as he observed that Tommy Head's conversion was real and lasting.

Andy began coming to a Sandhurst Thursday morning men's prayer breakfast, then held at Niko's restaurant. This breakfast began shortly after the founding of Heritage Church, first organized by Bob and Steve at a Shoney's restaurant on North Cashua Drive. The idea of the breakfast was to bring Christian men from around the city together for fellowship, prayer, and exhortation, regardless of their church affiliation. It continues today. Over the years, it became mostly a Sandhurst function, but even today, folks from two other local churches come regularly. Leadership started with Steve Imbeau, then Mike Roberts, then Harry Lyles for a very short time, then Pastor Bob, then Wick Jackson and sometimes Greg Stuckey, back to Pastor Bob, and now Ron Bennett. It grew from the original twelve to about forty and now back to about fourteen. We also moved around among local restaurants: from Shoney's then to Bazen's then to the Eat More Again (later renamed Deno's) then to Niko's, then back to Bazen's, and now to the Venus. The original start time was 6:00 a.m., and is now 6:30 a.m., running for about one hour.

To some of the breakfast regulars, curious why he was coming, Andy Anderson explained he was exploring Christianity by swimming alongside or even up to the side of the "boat." He asked us not to preach to him, but to pray for him and with him. And he kept coming to breakfast on Thursday mornings. After about a year, one Thursday morning he announced, "I am in the boat." And everybody cheered and clapped. Carol later joined him "in the boat." They really *were* in the boat, as the old life melted away. Andy couldn't help but talk to his friends and strangers about Jesus. He loved to start his prayers with, "Good morning, God," or, "How are you, God?"—he just couldn't help but be non-traditional, and we loved him for it. He continued his music gigs and worked gospel messages into his song sets. He was particularly fond of the Guthrie Family music, and even though based on anti-establishment poetry, the Guthrie music could be adapted to Christian purpose.

Andy developed colon cancer, and even with aggressive therapy, died in 2007. Knowing he was ready to die, he gave away his tools and supplies. But more importantly, he prepared a personal farewell video on a CD to be played at his funeral and then distributed. He themed it around the transformation of his old life, Guthrie music, and the gospel. He probably thus reached more people for the Christian gospel dead than he did alive.

We visited Grace Calcutt about once a quarter when she was with her daughter, Becky Ford, and less often when she moved to the Southland Health Care Center. Grace was a remarkable woman; she was Sandhurst's prayer warrior and more. She maintained a current list of Sandhurst members and friends and prayed for them routinely. She called most of them by phone just to "check on them" or when she heard there was illness or troubles. She called Shirley during her cancer chemotherapy and also called when she heard Charles was having trouble. She sent Christmas and birthday cards, the birthday cards often humorous. She sent handwritten letters to the Sandhurst missionaries, maintaining a current list. She made sure to get the lists of all the participants from all the Sandhurst short-term missionary trips.

Her missionary letters were important, asking about their health and families, but also writing some theology and Christian encouragement, and always with some money wrapped up in a separate paper: one dollar, two dollars, and sometimes five dollars. Never very much, but what she could afford, and sometimes these small amounts were *all* of her savings on hand. Missionaries later told us, often with tears in their eyes, that they preserved her letters as almost "holy documents" and couldn't spend the money, it was too precious. Grace was indeed an embodiment of the widow with her mites (see Luke 21:1–4). There has yet been none like her or to replace her. Yet she had humor and loved political jokes. And believe it or not, she was a dedicated Clemson football fan, wearing full Clemson colors when watching Clemson football games on TV or listening by radio!

Grace died on October 10, 2019.

About once or twice a year we visited with JoAnne McLaurin, better known as "Lady Bug." The nickname was from her wild days, but she kept it after her conversion, and she had lots of Lady Bug paraphernalia around her home and car. She put a red band on her auto antenna, but this also helped her find her car. She is notable at Sandhurst for her service. She loves to deliver food—one dinner at a time—to folks who are recently home from the hospital or otherwise ill, who are home with a new baby, or otherwise would have trouble preparing a decent family meal. Over the years, she developed the Sandhurst "Sunshine Committee" (unofficial name) with many helpers. Her favorite meals include butter beans, coleslaw, ham or chicken, macaroni and cheese, and sweet iced tea with corn bread and sometimes sweet potatoes—traditional Southern country cooking. She also loves to cook a meal of cornbread and vegetable soup. The Norrises and the Imbeaus have received several deliveries of both meals over the years, always much loved and appreciated.

But she does more. In a humorous but appreciative spirit, many of the Sandhurst family still call her "Reverend Lady Bug." She tries to talk to each newcomer on Sunday Mornings, if only a "hello." And she gives out licorice candy, her favorite vitamin, before Sunday services. She is the Sandhurst happiness lady and more important than she probably knows.

Lady Bug also went the extra mile when an ill Harold Morris came back to Florence for two months in the midst of medical evaluation for Multiple Endocrine Disorder with a combination of diabetes and thyroid disorder. She was a trouper amid his pain, suffering, and boredom. Of note, David Brown, Andy Anderson, and Dale Baker were very solicitous of Harold during that time, even driving him back and forth from Georgia.

We often detoured on Tuesday nights to one of the hospitals to visit a Sandhurst member or Sandhurst friend when they were a patient in the hospital or emergency room. Once, one of the patients was Robbie Norris, Bob's son, with a severe asthma attack. Bob was basically a full-time hospital visitor and counselor. He often visited folks in one of the two Florence hospitals who were not connected to Sandhurst because of a request, to be friendly and caring but also to offer human assistance or some gospel. And the same with his counseling, usually marriage counseling. Folks came to him from the city, the region, the state, and even the nation. Bob not only had the spiritual gift of teaching, pastoring, and evangelism, but he was also a gifted counselor. In fact, counseling may have been his most important work of all.

Sandhurst continues an important counseling ministry. Revees Cannon, the executive pastor, began a professional counseling ministry that evolved into the iHope Christian Care and Counseling Center where Reeves serves as a licensed professional counselor (LPC). Reeves received his undergraduate degree from Columbia International University in youth ministry. He later graduated with honors from Dallas Theological Seminary with a master of arts in biblical counseling. He is a member of the American Association of Christian Counselors and a board-certified professional Christian counselor with the International Board of Christian Counselors. Reeves is certified in both Prepare-Enrich and SYMBIS, which are the leading pre-marriage and marriage assessments. Reeves is passionate about marriage and family relationships. He believes that the family is an integral part of a healthy society and he has devoted much of his professional life to working with families within a counseling context. When Reeves is not at church, he enjoys hanging with Rebecca and their three children at the lake, beach, or just in the backyard. On occasion, Reeves will compete in Olympic-distance triathlons and he is an avid fan of the University of South Carolina.

For a time, Sandhurst also supported a Christian family counseling ministry in Dublin, Ireland. Mary Ann Steffy helped Bob establish Sandhurst when he first came over to Florence to hold meetings in the Sandhurst neighborhood: she provided the song and music inspiration. She frequently visited the new Sandhurst (Heritage Church) on Sundays and often gave special concerts, partly as fundraisers. She moved to Ireland about ten years later. Mary Ann developed metastatic breast cancer and died in Ireland in 2016. Along the cancer path, she developed special relationships with Diane Sansbury, Barbara Alexander, Marianne Laing, and Shirley Imbeau, among others.

For the first ten years or so, we would also stop by the Church at Sandhurst's sports teams' games on Tuesday nights in season: basketball and baseball. We would visit with the team and fans, usually mixing around to chat and sometimes sitting for a while in the stands or bleachers. Sometimes we would help at the concession stands.

An unexpected incident at one of the basketball games had a positive impact. Going in for a layup, an aggressive Chip Register was hit by at least one swinging elbow and fell to the floor bleeding. We rushed over and made sure he was conscious and not badly injured, and then tried to stop his nosebleed with towels. But it would not stop, or only temporarily. We decided to take him to the emergency room and so Bob and I bundled him up for the trip to McLeod where his nose was cauterized, and he stopped bleeding. Well, that sort of bonded us and we remained friends until the Registers moved on to Columbia, South Carolina. Chip and I had been sort of competitive. I was in his Sunday school class, but this emergency thing changed his thinking about me: I was no longer a physician, but now just a regular guy.

The Registers had once served in France as missionaries and found the missions emphasis at Sandhurst important and refreshing.

Heritage and Sandhurst were always dedicated to Christian missions. In fact, from the beginning, all non-designated receipts were split one-third to missionary work. The church had a very active missions committee headed in turn by Steve

Adams, Gregg Stuckey, Jeff Crane, David Brown, Kristi Tellis, and Tim Bokelman.

While visiting on Tuesday nights, we also tried to visit each missions couple leaving from Sandhurst and Florence a month or so before their departure, to pray, encourage, just talk, and show support. These couples included Kirk and Marianne Laing (Italy), Gregg and Jamie Stuckey (Belize), Wick and Cindy Jackson (Ethiopia and Bolivia), Tommy and Angela Head (Peru), and Caleb and Louise King (Kenya). Others who were not visited by us before leaving but at other times or in our homes, including Paul and Robin Johnson (Peru), Timmy and Kenyon Powers (Ukraine), Kathie Koerwer (Wycliffe Bible Translators), and the Jamie Lucas family. Both the Jacksons and Kings are entrepreneurial and engineering types and these skills or traits expressed themselves in important projects in their mission assignments.

After our visiting years were over, but also from Sandhurst, Nicky Cloyes, Jonathan Fulmer, and Joel Bokelman went to work with OM Ships. Skip and Tami Bachman are bound for the Dominican Republic; Tami is Paul and Robin Johnson's daughter.

Local Florence missions connected to Sandhurst include House of Hope, the East Florence Mission, Child Evangelism Fellowship, A Choice 2 Make, and Good News Clubs. We did visit the House of Hope and the East Florence Mission one Tuesday evening each.

Beginning about 1995, we invited some of the couples we visited on Tuesday nights to Beauzimbo Farm in Darlington County for dinner with the Norrises and Imbeaus. Typically, the couples were those we visited on a Tuesday night who then started attending at Sandhurst for at least a couple of months. Beauzimbo was a hundred-acre farm about twelve miles from Florence along the Old Hartsville Highway against Jeffries

Creek. A nice picnic area with shelter was carved out of the bank alongside a ten-acre pond, stocked with fish, bream and bass. So, it was a great site for a relaxing meal.

We invited different couples out there for a steak supper, usually two or three couples plus us four for a total of eight to ten folks, for a Thursday evening in the spring and fall, for six or seven dinners per year. We began about 1995 and ended when the Church at King Avenue began meeting on Thursday evenings. The Modus Operandi was usually about the same: Shirley would ride out with Anne and Bob to set up and give Bob some fishing time. The guests and Steve would come about 6:30 p.m. (Steve came in from Myrtle Beach, as Thursday was his "beach day"). Anne and Bob would bring salad and dessert, and Shirley brought steaks, corn, and hors d'oeuvre. We would sit along the lake or in the shed for appetizers and conversation and then cook the steaks and corn. We would try to end by about 8:30 p.m. or even earlier. These were always great evenings and a great bonding experience for the new Sandhurst family folks, allowing them to come to know the pastor.

Bob loved to fish and often fished off the dock waiting for the Thursday evening guests to arrive, usually catching something. But once he "caught" a water moccasin, sleeping under the canoe, around his leg. He was fishing along the bank and the canoe was tipped over along the edge of the grassy bank. When Bob accidentally bumped into the canoe, he surprised the snake, resting under the dark and cool side of the tipped canoe, who then attacked his shoe and leg. Bob yelled out, "A snake, a snake is around my leg." Shaken, Anne's horror could only be expressed in a scream, then joined by Shirley who hated all snakes. Somehow, Bob successfully wrestled it back into the water without injury to either. We never knew if it was great skill, blind luck, or God's grace, but Bob expertly grabbed the moccasin by the head and arched its flopping body into the lake.

Beginning about the year 2000, the Adamses and Imbeaus began alternating early June church picnics with activities for all ages, including fishing, hiking, swimming, volleyball, football, and baseball. The emphasis was on the children and, of course, eating. After several years, these picnics were mostly at Beauzimbo Farm. Later, after the Lynn Browns bought a place about three miles from Beauzimbo, the church picnics were moved to the Browns's farm. These summer picnics gradually faded away as the church body became too large for a group picnic day, but they provided great memories of the "old days."

Stories Along the Way:
Cultural Insights

*"But when he saw the multitudes, he was
moved with compassion on them, because
they fainted, and were scattered abroad, as
sheep having no shepherd."* MATTHEW 9:36

*"And there are diversities of operations,
but It Is the same God which worketh
all in all . . . To another the working of
miracles; to another prophecy; to another
discerning of spirits."* 1 CORINTHIANS 12:6,10A

*"Be not carried about with divers and
strange doctrines. For it is a good thing
that the heart be established
with grace."* HEBREWS 13:9A

SINCE THE TEMPERANCE MOVEMENT, alcohol has become a controversial topic in Southern Christian circles. Traditionally, Catholics, Presbyterians, and Anglicans (Episcopal) drink at least wine. The Southern Baptists usually do not drink alcohol publicly and can be strident about it.

Alcohol use is throughout the Bible, usually wine and usually at special occasions. Some of the Old Testament covenants were struck with the seal of alcohol. Even when God met the

Hebrew leaders on Sinai, drink (alcohol) was provided. Jacob's son, Benjamin, was arrested when security found the regent's wine cup in his grain bag and, of course, one of Joseph's cellmates was the palace wine steward. David notes in several of his poems the symbolism of wine to represent both joy (the early alcohol effect) and pain (the stomping of the grapes).

The Jewish Passover provides several wine courses, and of course, Jesus used one of them to commemorate the upcoming shedding of his own blood in the Last Supper, taken at a normal Passover supper, recalling the Davidic imagery of mixed joy and suffering. In fact, the Jewish leaders had already accused Jesus of drinking too much wine, but many appreciated his "water to wine" miracle at the beginning of his ministry (John 2). In that instance, when Jewish weddings sometimes spreading out over two to three weeks, the groom's father noted that the wine from Jesus was much better than all the previous wine.

The modern Baptist argument that the ancient wines were somehow dilute, or inferior, or really just grape concentrate is, of course, rendered false by these examples and recorded history. History provides testament to the excellence of Mediterranean and Middle Eastern wines. Even in the New Testimony epistles, Paul and Peter speak of reasonable wine use for health and social occasion, but both warn against drunkenness.

Anyway, the topic of alcohol often came up on Tuesday nights, particularly at the beginning years when Sandhurst was a new church in Florence. Florence is also a small town, and many folks had probably already seen us out to dinner with filled wine glasses, particularly the Imbeaus. Bob had a great answer to this and similar questions about dress, movies, and dancing. He began by explaining that Sandhurst held certain immutable truths printed in the doctrinal statement that could not be compromised, and that most other biblical lifestyle or dietary issues (what he called "non-essential" issues) were left to individual conscience. Paul was careful in Corinthians and Romans to urge the folks who believed a certain way on social or dietary issues not to take offense from the contrary, nor to force their philosophy on others.

Several times, we encountered wine bottles set out or beer boxes on the floor. We reassured the nervous folks as best we could with Bob using our personal example of dinner wine, but also his story of mowing the lawn on a hot day and enjoying and appreciating a "cool one" at job's end. Bob loved the quip, "Jesus turned water to wine, and some Christians have been working ever since to turn it back to water." And those who did not like our take on alcohol, well there are many fine Baptist or Independent Baptist churches in Florence, too. Several times a year, we came upon folks who had already had too much alcohol that evening; we asked them about a better visiting date.

The topic of angels and angelic worship came up surprisingly often. The issue was sometimes simple, "Do you believe in angels?" "Yes." But often more complex, as folks worked into the discussion mythology, mysticism, angelic worship, and their personal angels. To be sure, angels are certainly biblical and numerous in both testaments. Typically, they are used as messengers to mankind: Hagar, Abraham, Jacob, Moses, Joshua, Elijah, Jason, Samuel, Mary, Zechariah (both Testaments), Paul, Peter, and John, and others if you count visions; sometimes as warriors: the Egyptian Passover night of death, the siege of Samaria, the Old Testament Arab wars, Jesus's crucifixion, and in Revelation; and sometimes as guardians: Balaam, Babylon, Jesus, and Mary, or helpers: Peter and a general mention of angels as the helpers of believers in the new testament (Hebrews 1:14).

The Bible does not hide that there are also angels adverse to God, particularly Satan's angels and the angels chained under the Euphrates River (see Revelation 9:14). Several of these angels and demons are probably named in the Bible as well as Satan. We think that Baal, Bel, Moloch, Ashtaroth (Baal's consort), and Ishtar were probably angels, although this is somewhat controversial since some scholars think these were just the names of common local city or regional idols or even a slang for Canaanite idols. However, the secular scholar Will Durant translates both Baal and Allah as "god/lord of the earth/soil." The equivalence of Baal and Allah would not surprise us. Some also interpret Baal as "god/lord of the sun," which places him right alongside Satan, which would not surprise us either. See *The Age of Faith*, pages 155–344, and *Our Oriental Heritage*, pages 299–349.

Angels usually appear in the Bible as normal people who can be touched and spoken to, but occasionally as cherubim with two wings each (the Garden of Eden and the Ark of the Covenant) or seraphim with multiple wings or wheels (the visions of Isaiah and Ezekiel). The angels at Jesus's birth in Matthew apparently appeared as people, but some hovered in the sky (later artists added the wings). Other than Baal and Ashtaroth, only four angels are specifically named in the Bible: the archangels Satan/Lucifer, Michael, Gabriel, and Raphael (Raphael is mentioned only in the Douay-Rheims translation of the Bible in the apocryphal book of Tobit).

As read by some, the early part of Genesis, and probably also Jude 1:6, implies that some angels deliberately gave up their place with God and immortality to marry women and have children. These fallen angels and offspring probably led to the longevity recorded before the Great Deluge (flood), as well as the advanced science and economy, together leading to the utter rejection of God (except for at least one family of Sethites) and then the desperate wickedness described in Genesis and early Romans, and then to the all-destroying flood. These lustful Genesis angels are probably the basis of the ancient pagan myths.

I will never forget the one night a young man went on and on about his personal angels, describing images befitting the *Piercing the Darkness* series by Frank Peretti. He was convinced that angels were meeting in his apartment complex or certainly nearby. We tried to point out that the theme of the novels was the power of prayer and the whole armor of God as described in Ephesians 6, probably not actual fighting bands of angels. Although, we acknowledged the reality of "spiritual warfare" (see Ephesians 6:10–18 and 1 Timothy 1:18).

We came across many other couples who were into angel worship and they wondered how we handled it; we referred them to the first several chapters of Hebrews, telling them we didn't, since we had no place for angel worship at all.

A common and perplexing issue was the rise of speaking in tongues and other sign gifts. Many devout Christians are convinced that they are not "complete" or "whole Christians" unless they speak in tongues. On the other hand, Sandhurst certainly holds to the spiritual gifts that build up and encourage the local church, including preaching, evangelism, prayer, exhortation, shepherding, helps, and the power of God to heal and sustain the human body. In the modern era, speaking in tongues probably began in a small Los Angeles church in the 1930s but has spread around the world and throughout the Christian church, whether Roman Catholic, Orthodox, or Protestant. It is often associated with Pentecostalism, but not limited to this one denomination. It has evolved into a kind of mysticism with special knowledge and skills, such as "angelic speech," "faith healing," and "special knowledge," including channeling. Emotional exuberance is often part of the service.

Indeed, several biblical figures probably spoke in human language not their own in the New Testament, and several leaders or prophets in the Old Testament had special powers, particularly Moses, Joshua, Elijah, and Elisha, but basically only these four. Most New Testament era folks spoke Greek and Aramaic, and the Jews also Hebrew, and the Romans also Latin; most educated folks knew all four languages. Philip probably did not need any special language powers to listen to and teach the Ethiopian in the desert; his transport was by the Holy Spirit, however.

But Peter's speech to the crowd on Pentecost Day was different. Probably about ten languages were represented, and Peter probably spoke in Aramaic, knowing the crowd. But the book of Acts says each person heard Peter in their own language. Peter did not *speak* in ten different languages. Rather, the Holy Spirit interpreted it for each person into their own language (in the modern world, as if Peter were at the United Nations), but Peter had no electronics nor human interpreters.

Long before Los Angeles, the Corinthians were speaking in tongues, not natural human language. Paul points out that such language is mischievous and certainly not helpful, since no one can understand it; it does no good to the rest of the congregation. And so, Paul says that such language has no place in the church unless at least two interpreters can agree as to the meaning (see 1 Corinthians 12–14). Note that Paul writes that love is the greatest spiritual gift of all, not tongues. In our view, Paul's requirement for two interpreters in agreement pretty much rules out angelic utterances or "speaking in tongues" in modern churches.

When asked about speaking in tongues, we would gently review the above understanding and history. Most folks were not convinced, but some came to change their view of the whole matter, and some even joined the Sandhurst family. We appreciate their enthusiasm and controlled exuberance at worship.

I will never forget the night one young lady was so into all "tongues" that when Bob came to his finishing prayer, she began a chant in an unknown language and he bravely and serenely continued on as if she were silent, but she continued in a louder and higher-pitched voice. I had trouble keeping a straight face but endured.

Another Tuesday night, while the Whittington Ministries was in Florence with a tent pitched up along Third Loop Road, we curiously stopped by at about 8:00 p.m. in summer twilight. And there was Jim Whittington in a white suit playing the piano just like in his TV ads; no speaking in tongues, yet. Folding chairs were set up on the field grass for about two hundred people, but only about fifty chairs were filled. Amusingly, as we walked up dressed in our typical business suits, two of Whittington handlers rushed up to us, even before we could get under the tent. They were polite but serious, asking, "Can we help you?" but before we could respond, they went on, "We don't want any trouble here tonight. Reverend Whittington is providing important spiritual guidance to these folks." I took the lead and laughed, saying, "Hey, relax, we are just curious bypassers who are actually out visiting tonight for a local church. We will not bother your service." And we turned around and left. But on the way home, we had a great conversation.

Legalism has plagued the church from the beginning. In fact, it is partially the cause of the original Council of Jerusalem (Acts 15). By legalism, we mean the introduction of laws and regulations into Christianity in order to direct behavior, akin to what existed under Judaism taken from Leviticus and Deuteronomy (and as amplified in the Talmud, the Gemara, and the Mishnah). Most believers would confirm that Christian salvation is through faith and grace based on God's great love through Jesus Christ, but then add the need for rules and regulations to live the Christian life. These folks have been called "Judaizers" because of the antecedent Mosaic Law, even though it was authored by God (see Galatians 3:25, "But after that faith is come, we are no longer under a schoolmaster").

Along the way comes the companion idea that good living, good Christian living, is the way to greater credit or even maintenance of original salvation. But we at Sandhurst disagree; we believe that Christian living is also through faith and grace with love. In our view, so-called "good works" are important and a sign of the Fruit of the Spirit (see Galatians 5:22), but *do not* bring salvation nor aid in salvation. The Roman Catholic Church brought faith and grace and good works together at the Council of Trent (beginning in 1543 to, in part, respond to Martin Luther), but in recent times have begun to retrace some of the Council. Anyway, scriptures in Romans, Galatians, and Ephesians serve to counter legalism, in our view.

And so of course, we ran into a variety of challenges about legalism, some already mentioned under the "alcohol vignette" above. Several other churches in Florence have criticized Sandhurst over the years for laxity on dress, appearance, or alcohol. And some of our visits were to folks then members of these churches. Many of our hosts appreciated our outreach and joined or continued in the Sandhurst family. But many did not; we always told them, "Sandhurst may not be for you, it is certainly not meant for everybody. We believe that God has a place for you, and it may not be Sandhurst. But we also want you to insist that Jesus is preached and that his salvation comes through faith and grace."

We always viewed it all as a bit humorous, but about once a year we crossed folks from these other churches visiting the same couples as we on the same Tuesday night. Once we joked with them, "It must be Tuesday night." I was astonished—but Bob was not—when couples would tell us straight out that they preferred rules and regulations, so that "they knew where they stood" and they appreciated defined "limits." Once, a lady actually went on and on about how she wanted a "cookie-cutter" church where the folks went about their business in a structured manner and so she would always know that "where she went in, is where she would come out." I was amused that some of her family were in leadership at Sandhurst.

Another thorny issue we faced visiting, particularly in the last decade, was the issue of divorce and cohabitation. Divorce rates fell during our visiting decades, but cohabitation increased so that by 2010, almost half of women under age 45 had lived with a man without marriage, accompanied by rising societal acceptance of almost 80 percent (from Wikipedia). For many years, Pastor Bob had a class at his home for the "single and single again" adults. As visitors, we faced the issue about once a month or so. Actually, as far as visiting goes, we ignored the phenomena unless brought up by the couple.

The biblical response to divorce and cohabitation is not, despite what some think, straightforward. God certainly did not originally intend for divorce, but eventually, Moses came to allow it, as pointed out to the Pharisees by Jesus himself (Deuteronomy 22:13 and Matthew 19:8) and Paul taught reconciliation if possible (1 Corinthians 7). Cohabitation is excluded in 1 Corinthians 7 and marriage encouraged. Most Protestant denominations have taken a firm stance against cohabitation without marriage in the modern era. When asked directly, we referred directly to these and other scriptures. We also presented the gospel as we always did, without any qualm.

Many times, we were asked about marriage. In fact, many times folks right off said, "We have been waiting for your visit. Will you marry us?" Or, "Will you marry us in your church?" The first step was to start off with the eighteen-wheeler truck accident story, but with Bob saying, "OK, but there is another issue I want to face first," and then respond just like he did for anybody else. With the typical time for answers or a gospel presentation and the knowledge of how they stood with Christianity, then then we went back to the original questions.

Bob would say, "The church part is easy. Any marriage in the church has to be approved by the elders. So, if that is what you want, then let us know, so we can put in a formal request." Bob then would go on, "The second part is also straightforward. I am licensed to perform marriages in South Carolina. I will marry either Christian couples or non-Christian couples, but not a mixed couple where one partner does not have assurance of salvation," adding, "and I require a private, counseling session before the marriage, probably best held as soon as possible." This straightforward approach resolved much anxiety and led to many conversions and eventual marriages.

The Last Word

"DAAG, GUM IT!!"
Bob Norris's favorite phrase, usually indicating pleasure or satisfaction or excited discovery.

APPENDIX

Postscript:
A Glimpse of One Special Trip

THE FIRST MAJOR NORRIS–IMBEAU trip was to Jerusalem and Italy to visit Sandhurst missionaries, the Laings. Friday, October 22, 1993: The bags are packed, goodbyes are said at the Florence airport, and we're off to Atlanta. Next stop, Paris!

Upon routine inspection of the passports, the sweet female French official observed, "Sir, your passport is expired." "Huh?" says Steve trying to awaken from his 2:00 a.m. (home time) stupor. Immediately, the reality of the situation sunk in and he telephoned using the airport gate agent's French phone card. When it seemed clear Steve was not going on to Jerusalem, Bob, Anne, and Shirley waved goodbye and sadly boarded the plane to Tel Aviv without him. Incredibly, only three minutes before takeoff, with the jet engines just whirling, he calmly walked onto the plane, grinning like a Cheshire cat. And in Tel Aviv, the duty officer allowed him into the country, providing he take care of getting a passport immediately. The secret of his conversations and arrangements will go to his grave—he says.

We had scheduled a tour for the next day to Masada. The bus took us past the caves of the Dead Sea Scrolls (the Qumran Ein Gedi caves—remember Ein Gedi? It's one of the places where David and King Saul met while Saul was chasing David) and past the lowest spot on the earth (400 meters below sea level). Masada was built on a rock hill by Herod the Great about 34 BC as a palace and fortress. Ben Eleazer with about six hundred Jewish zealots took refuge there for several years after the fall of Jerusalem (70 AD). The Romans built a wall around the rock with five fortified camps. After several years of futile siege, the Romans built a ramp up the west side of the rock. The indomitable followers of Eleazer saw only one end to their plight. They first burned all of Masada but the storehouses. And then each head of household killed his family and cast lots to determine the last Jew alive. When the Romans came through and over the wall, all the Jews were dead by their own hands—a hollow victory. The symbolism is very important for modern Israel. Many troops are inducted into the armed forces from atop Masada, and all school children must visit it at least once.

Nadine, our tour guide, persuaded us to visit the National Diamond Center where we had fun and bought some trinkets.

Nadine—Louise Imbeau look alike

Nadine grew up in South Africa and came to Israel to live on a kibbutz as part of the Zionist Movement. She met an Egyptian Jew, left the kibbutz, married, and settled down permanently in Israel to raise a family. She looks exactly like Louise Imbeau, Steve's sister.

The next day, we set out to tour in earnest. First, we spent four hours in the Israel Museum. The museum preserves the archeological and traditional history of Israel and the Jewish peoples in and out of Palestine. Bob and Steve had a great time making their own observations and asking the guide difficult questions. There is one artifact probably from Solomon's Temple (an ivory pomegranate). The typical findings from the Assyrian conquest of Israel (the Northern Kingdom) are preserved. Somewhat more is available from Herod's Temple since the true Second Temple of Ezra and Nehemiah was profaned by the Greeks. The Jews often don't refer to it. We viewed photos of and artifacts from synagogues around the world, items used in Shabbat, and booths used in the Feast of Tabernacles (Sukkot).

Classic

The Dead Sea Scrolls exhibit is solemn. We saw the book of Isaiah wrapped around the inner walls of the circular building, parts of Deuteronomy, along with well-preserved military orders, household inventories, and shopping lists. The biblical texts were copied by the Essenes. The docents pointed out that the Torah had to be reviewed three times after copied to ensure accuracy. The Israel Museum also had a special Chagall exhibit. Only his "Jewish" and Zionist works were on display. Marc Chagall is famous for his grand use of color and sweeping motion. Unfortunately, his "gentile works" were not displayed (the UN windows, the St. Stephen's windows, his prints, etc.).

We turned aside into a private Jewish museum dedicated to the Third Temple close to the Wailing Wall. The Third Temple is planned, of course, not built; necessary furniture and garments are already all prepared and in waiting. They call it the Third Temple since Nehemiah's was profaned by the Greeks and so Herod's Temple is called the Second Temple. Models of the proposed new temple were all around, plus several models of the Tabernacle, Solomon's Temple, Solomon's Throne Room (St. Peter's Basilica in Rome is based on this), and Noah's Ark. All the historical models were biblically accurate.

We engaged many Jews in discussion of the new temple. Most
would shrug and go to another conversation, although some
believed in it and looked forward to it, but most didn't care or
didn't believe in it.

The Wailing Wall

We walked down a well-guarded staircase to the plaza
in front of the Western Wall (the Wailing Wall). This wall includes stones from Herod's Temple. Bob and Steve went into
a small, men-only synagogue to the left of the wall where the
wall was excavated down another fifty to a hundred feet (indicating even greater age). Guards prevented us from walking
along a tunnel path behind the synagogue. Officials who we
asked about the tunnel and excavation would only shrug and
just smiled when we asked if this wall could in part go back
to Solomon's time (maybe). We later found out that this tunnel
was designed to go under the Temple Mount. We prayed and
got photographed at the Wailing Wall. Thousands of small pa-
pers are stuck in the wall with written prayers.

We bumped into Nadine again, and she directed us to
the Via Dolorosa—the Way of Agony to the Cross (literally,
the Avenue of Suffering)—walked by Jesus on his last day

in Jerusalem (for now). Of course, remember, the city was burned to the ground in 70 AD by the Romans, but Jesus did carry his cross through the streets of Jerusalem in the same general area. We walked up these steps for a mile or two and finally turned aside at St. Stephen's Gate where we found our two wise men, as if from Proverbs 31 (actually, just Bob and Steve). Along the way, we shopped in several Arab shops (the Old City is divided into the Arab, Jewish, Armenian, and Catholic Quarters). Arabs love to bargain but can be too persistent. We found some excellent trinkets and gifts.

Across the street was purportedly Golgotha and the Garden Tomb. Golgotha is only a few yards from the Old City through what used to be called the Dung Gate (now St. Stephen's Gate). In Jesus's day, it was a quarry and a Jewish place of stoning; the Romans used it as a crucifixion site for the poor (the Place of the Skull since, with some imagination, the stone face looks like a human skull). Now it is an Arab bus terminal. Nearby, some archaeologists in 1867 discovered an old vineyard with a huge cistern (400,000 liters) and later discovered an old hewed tomb for two. Some now believe that this was Joseph of Arimathea's garden (vineyard) and Jesus's tomb. The evidence

The Garden Tomb, tourist card photo

JERUSALEM

THE
GARDEN
TOMB

is good, but the traditional Roman Catholic site at the Church of the Holy Sepulcher was established back in about 330 AD. The Golgotha tomb area is now in the hands of a Protestant Christian group from England, the Garden Tomb (Jerusalem) Association since 1894 with legal standing both in England and Israel. The tomb is large and so the stone must have been huge, indeed. "He is not here, but is risen" (Luke 24:6a). Many Christians come here now to take the Lord's Supper and meditate. We were touring the Garden Tomb at the same time as Hal Lindsey and his tour were meeting for Communion; we joined their Communion service and chatted with him briefly.

The next day started by finally getting Steve's new passport and then back to the Temple Mount for a final try at the Dome of the Rock (again closed). Now we went up to the top of

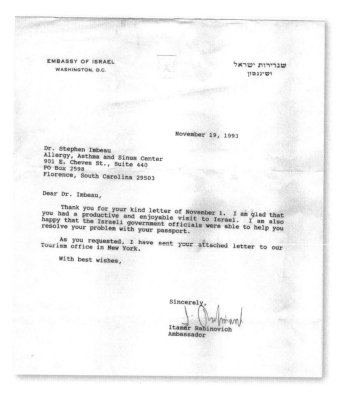

the Mount of Olives where we could stand where Jesus went up to heaven and where he will again come down to touch earth. We could look out at the Eastern Gate with an Arab cemetery in front as an attempt to keep Jesus out (the Arabs think he will be a Levitical priest and therefore cannot cross a cemetery). The gate is walled over as prophesied by Jesus, but of course, will be again open someday. Many Jews are also buried nearby so that they can be close to the Messiah on his appearance. The brook Kidron runs between the Mount of Olives and the city wall.

Cabbie Abe (born in Brooklyn) took us to a panoramic view of the city and—lo and behold—there were camels for hire (Shirley's next Christmas card). Steve went first and the guide had to fling him up onto the camel. The camel had been agitated by a passing bus and tried to bite Steve's left shoulder. The camel also blew up its tongue to make a very strange noise that only Anne could mimic. Then the camel began to stand, forcing Steve to do an incredible balancing act, and then on to the ride. Shirley was next, then, in turn, Bob and Anne, and then both together. The guide literally threw Shirley up onto the camel with her skirt flying (hard to be modest on camel-back). Trying to cover the legs and hold on to the saddle all at the same time was tough. Anne too was thrown atop the beast. Bob made it all look easy and several nearby tourists thought he looked just like an original camel driver. Great pictures with us on a camel overlooking Jerusalem. What fun!

Abe was not as much fun as we next rode to Bethlehem (basically a suburb of Jerusalem). We could tell he was not keen on going there (it's an Arab city and had some recent incidents). The ancient town so significant to Christian believers has become dirty, filled with graffiti, and overrun with mean-spirited people. A tremendous church, the Church of the Nativity, was built at the site of the grotto manger and a silver star marks the supposed site of Jesus's birth. It was still wonderful to be at least near where "the Word was made flesh, and dwelt among us" (John 1:14a) and where "she brought forth her firstborn son . . . and laid him in a manger" (Luke 2:7). These verses are written in the church. But we left quickly when some bystanders told Shirley that they didn't like Americans (she forgot to tell them she was Canadian).

The Laings and Bob Norris

The next day, we were on to visit the Laings in Italy.

What a treat to see Kirk Laing at the Florence, Italy, train station after our flight from Israel and train trip from Rome. After retrieving our luggage, we headed for the Florentine hills along a winding road to Kirk's six-hundred-year-old Liechti (Marianne was a Liechti) manor house (the Laings live in only a small part of it, lower level). Italians drive their small cars very fast, but even so, the Laings live about an hour from Florence. What a view! What charm! And what a delight to hug sweet Marianne in her family home in her own country. After some espresso, we went down to the village of Scarperia.

Scarperia is a beautiful old Italian town. We enjoyed having Marianne show off her town and introducing us to her friends. Back up in the hills, we watched Kirk and Marianne prepare a meal of shish kebab (sausage, turkey, pork, bay leaf, and bread) visiting with some of Marianne's upstairs Liechti family, several staying to have dinner with us. You see, Marianne grew up in this house. Before dinner, we enjoyed wine, bread, and dried tomatoes with olive oil with the visitors.

Philippe and David were excited to see us when they got back from basketball practice and enjoyed their gifts, but we sort of lost them when they began to watch *Pete's Dragon* and eat pizza. Kirk had achieved local fame for his basketball—even in the newspapers. About ten to fifteen enthusiastic young people arrived after dinner to meet the Americans. They love Kirk and Marianne and studying the Bible, and often sang together. (We sang with them, too. And Bob tried to teach some new songs.) But Kirk and Marianne must also face their deep Catholic tradition and the local priest. While Pastor Bob spent the next evening in counseling and prayer with the Laing family, Anne and the Imbeaus went for dinner to the fabulous Les Borodino restaurant in Florence, Bob going up to Scarperia alone that afternoon.

Florence is an ancient city that was controlled from about 1315 to 1850 by the Medici family. The Medicis started in banking and went into trade. They helped to invent the concepts of mercantile insurance and double-entry bookkeeping. The family's fortune was founded by Averardo de Medici and the first famous member was Cosimo (Cosimo became the family head in 1428; in 1434, Cosimo became the most powerful person in all Florence—after being released from jail and exile). For a time, the Medici controlled the Catholic Church (Popes Leo X, Clement VII, Pius IV, and Leo XI) and thus much of Europe. The Medici homes are incredible for their size, architecture, and artwork. Most of their property now belongs to the state, although the Bormeo and Borghese families have bought some of the properties. The Pitti and Uffizi were their enemies for much of the Middle Ages. Despite all this wealth and power, the Medici family suffered from hereditary gout.

Friday morning, we went back to the Pitti and Uffizi palaces (previously closed by a strike; Italian labor strikes are selective and usually specific by day or hour). Bob tried to be like "Waldo" and explore an off-limits section of the palace but got stopped short by an irate watchman. The Patti's rooms have

Michelangelo's David

individual themes and were painted by different artists (usually the ceilings—the Italians cannot tolerate a plain ceiling); the themes are typically biblical or mythical. The Uffizi has many old masters donated to the state by the Medici.

We trekked across town to an old monastery that is now a museum of Michelangelo's work, including his David statue. This statue looks alive and is marvelous (although Bob noted that the real David would have been circumcised). We stopped for lunch and then off to the market where we found gorgeous Italian fabric for the Imbeaus' front hall. Florence is a beautiful, clean, prosperous, and sophisticated city.

At 7:00 p.m., Kirk and Marianne arrived for dinner and the night over with us at the Hotel Pitti de Ponte Vecchio (sorry, the hotel, not the palace). We had a good time together and they looked very romantic together. Marianne skipped through the streets like a child, showing us all her favorite places. Our first pick of restaurants was filled so we went back to Les Borodino for another great Italian meal. Saturday morning, Marianne took us shopping at some of the normal department stores. Sadly, we had to say goodbye but look forward to seeing them again this next summer in Florence, South Carolina.

Once back in Rome, we went to Giovanni's for our last Italian meal and then took a bus tour around Rome (ancient and modern) until about midnight. The Trevi Fountain is majestic and nearby we had some delicious Italian ice cream. The highlights of the tour included some of Trajan's Wall, the Colosseum, the Vatican, the Venice Palace, the Roman Forum (and the other forums nearby), Garibaldi Square (on top of Janus Hill), the Circus Maximus (where the Christians were made sport of), and the Church of the Holy Mother (Marie Magnum), which was the largest church in Rome before St. Peter's was built (the pagan shrines were relatively small compared to the Christian churches. Sadly, the Christians removed or destroyed much of the ancient art and sculpture). Lastly, we viewed the monument to the Italian Independent State honoring Victorio II.

The next morning, we went to the Vatican and St. Peter's Basilica; the complex is staggering. St. Peter's was designed

The two couples in 2004

to compete with Solomon's Temple and it does (far bigger, but with less gold). Shirley and Anne wanted to pose with the Swiss Guards. We toured the interior, passing tombs of popes and saints. We tried to tour the Sistine Chapel, but the line was three hours long (it was a Sunday morning, plus it had just re-opened after some renovations). Then a long flight home.

About the Authors

STEPHEN A. IMBEAU was born on November 25, 1947, on the wrong coast, in Portland, Oregon, growing up in Oakland, California. His parents were told to expect mental retardation since he was born with severe fetal distress, but they were pleasantly surprised when he met the childhood milestones, some even early. His father was a machinist for the Hyster Company, a subsidiary of the Caterpillar Company, and went on to become a salesman.

Imbeau grew up as a nerd, with absolutely no athletic ability at all, not dating until age 19, a junior in college. He attended college at the University of California at Berkeley in mathematics and computer science and then medical school at the University of California at San Francisco, graduating with a Doctor of Medicine degree in May of 1973. He completed both internship and residency in Internal medicine at the University of Wisconsin in 1977 and Allergy Fellowship in June 1979.

He married Shirley Ruth Burke of Toronto, Canada, in Toronto on August 18, 1979. In February, they left Wisconsin to come to Florence, arriving March 1, 1980, to three inches of snow, joining Dr. Peter Williams allergy practice. The first five years or so were tumultuous; after a few twists and turns, Imbeau began his own allergy practice in Florence as the first Board Certified Allergist in the region. The practice grew and grew and grew as he moved from independent practice to the Carolina Health Care Group to the Pee Dee Internal Medicine Group, and then with Dr. Joseph Moyer founded the Allergy, Asthma & Sinus Center in 1996.

In 1984, he became the president of the Florence County Medical Society and joined the board of the South Carolina Medical Association in 1986, becoming its president in 1998. Early medical mentors in Florence included Drs. Frank Boysia, Hans Habemeir, Bill Hester, and Steve Ross; later Drs. Bruce White, Eddie Floyd, and Louis Wright also helped his medico-political career.

He got involved with the Florence Community first through the American Lung Association, the Big Brothers, the local medical review organization (PSRO), then the Florence Symphony, becoming president of the Symphony for six years, first in 1994. He joined the Chamber of Commerce Board and the Florence County Progress becoming chairman of County Progress in 1993. He became active in Mayor Frank Willis' campaign and worked closely with the mayor throughout his term and beyond.

He also developed a career at the American Medical Association (AMA), becoming alternate delegate to the AMA from South Carolina in 1996. He left South Carolina for a time to work at AMA with the American Academy of Allergy, Asthma, and Immunology, returning to the South Carolina Delegation at AMA in 2004. He became chair of the South Carolina Delegation in 2007 until 2015. In 2013, he became chairman of the Southeastern Delegation to AMA for two years; also, in 2011 he became Chair of the Elections Committee, and editor of the SED Newsletter in 2011, both offices continuing. He is also now the Chair of the American Medical Political Action Committee.

For more about Stephen and his writing, please visit *stephenaimbeau.com*.

ROBERT A. NORRIS was born on April 7, 1938, in London, Ontario. He grew up in London, turning to his wild nature after his mother died in a car accident; he moved in with his grandmother when his father could no longer provide discipline and decided to turn Bob over to her. Eventually, he became a Christian through his grandmother's faithfulness and prayers. He decided to go to Columbia Bible College after high school, but after an interview in Columbia, decided to work instead, but came back a year later with Les Hobbins, where Anne Russell was still a student. Anne and Bob were married June 2, 1961, in Sumter.

Graduating in 1962, Anne and Bob then moved around a bit as he became a pastor: to Charlotte at Calvary Presbyterian Church, then to Chicago to study music, then to Shreveport, Louisiana, at the Coventry Baptist Church, then to the Liberty Baptist Church in Appomattox, Virginia, then to the Long Branch Baptist Church in Sumter, then to join the Canadian Barry Moore's evangelism crusade as director of music, then back to Sumter to be the lead pastor at the Harmony Church for many years. Finally, a brief stay in Atlanta followed by a long stay in Florence.

Rob and Deb Colones—Rob was saved through Bob's former Sumter Harmony Church—were trying to start a Bible fellowship church in Florence along with Dr. Steve and Ann Adams and Bob and Vickye Hinshelwood. Starting in late 1984, Bob came over from Sumter to hold weekly Bible studies and hymn sings in the couples' homes and later also in Marianne and Kirk Laing's home to evaluate local Florence interest, breaking those off when Bob and Anne moved to Atlanta.

As the home studies grew and grew, even in the absence of Pastor Bob, the three founding couples realized it was time for more. They wanted to start an evangelical Christian church in Florence with an emphasis on evangelism, on Christian living with growth in Christian understanding and individual development, and on missions. In faith, the Norrises moved to Florence from Atlanta in 1986 at Rob Colones's request, thus founding the Heritage Church (Rob Colones became chairman of the elders), later to become the Church at Sandhurst in 1990. The new church had both a board of elders and a deacon board. The three founding couples all lived in or near the Heritage neighborhood in Florence, thus the name of the new church, the Heritage Church.

Acknowledgments

WE MUST ACKNOWLEDGE our wives who put up with us all these years and faithfully supporting the visitation ministry, but, as they would readily admit, also enjoyed our dinners out, our times together, our trips, and our close friendship. We want to thank Pastor Adam Richardson and all the folks who helped to edit the manuscript, who contributed to the Great Stories vignettes, who provided sound advice along the way as well as the book testimonials. We thank all the elders, deacons, and members of the Church at Sandhurst who have over the years provided the framework for these efforts and who have poured themselves with prayer and love into our lives. A special thanks to Pastor Ronnie Stevens and Paul and Robin Johnson for their important contributions to this book and our lives. We particularly thank all the Florentines who graciously invited us into their homes over the years. And we thank you, our readers.

We also appreciate the Credo House Publishers team: Tim Beals, Pete Ford, and Sharon VanLoozenoord. And we thank book consultant Chad Allen. Well done, all.

Stephen Imbeau and Robert Norris, 2021

Photo Credits

All photos by Shirley Imbeau unless otherwise marked

1. Steve Imbeau and Bob Norris
2. Steve Imbeau and Bob Norris
3. Church at Sandhurst
4. Church at Sandhurst
5. Church at Sandhurst
6. YMCA entrance
7. Weight room, from depositphotos by Wavebreakmedia
8. Church at Sandhurst logo (from the church by email)
9. Venn diagram, by Stephen Imbeau
10. Columbia International University entrance, by bestpsychologydegrees.com, ciu.edu
11. Classic
12. Nadine
13. The Wailing Wall and Bob Norris
14. The Garden Tomb
15. Ambassador's letter
16. The Laings and Bob Norris
17. Michelangelo's David
15. The two couples, by a Greenbriar Hotel employee

Made in the USA
Columbia, SC
27 May 2021

38061127R00060